INSPIRE TO LIVE NOW

"Breaking Free from Emotional Shackles"

Dede Shepherd, PhD

TEACH Services, Inc.
PUBLISHING
www.TEACHServices.com • (800) 367-1844

World rights reserved. This book or any portion thereof may not be copied or reproduced in any form or manner whatever, except as provided by law, without the written permission of the publisher, except by a reviewer who may quote brief passages in a review.

The author assumes full responsibility for all contents of this book and permissions therefor, including layout, design, and the accuracy of all facts and quotations as cited herein. The opinions expressed in this book are the author's personal views and interpretations, and do not necessarily reflect those of the publisher.

This book is provided with the understanding that the publisher is not engaged in giving spiritual, legal, medical, or other professional advice. If authoritative advice is needed, the reader should seek the counsel of a competent professional.

Copyright © 2025 DeDe Shepherd, PhD
Copyright © 2025 TEACH Services, Inc.
ISBN-13: 9781479616695 (Paperback)
ISBN-13: 9781479616701 (ePub)
Library of Congress Control Number: 2025905026

All scripture quotations, unless otherwise indicated, are taken from King James Version. Public domain.

All Scripture references marked (NKJV) are taken from the New King James Version® of the Bible, copyright © 1982 by Thomas Nelson. Used by permission. All rights reserved.

All Scripture references marked ASV are taken from the American Standard Version of the Bible. Public domain.

All Scripture references marked EASY are taken from the EasyEnglish Bible, Copyright © MissionAssist 2019 - Charitable Incorporated Organisation 1162807. Used by permission. All rights reserved.

Scripture quotations marked ESV are taken from The Holy Bible, English Standard Version. ESV® Text Edition: 2016. Copyright © 2001 by Crossway Bibles, a publishing ministry of Good News Publishers.

All Scripture references marked MEV are taken from The Holy Bible, Modern English Version, copyright © 2014 by Military Bible Association. Published and distributed by Charisma House.

All Scripture references marked NIV are taken from the Holy Bible, New International Version®, NIV®, copyright © 1973, 1978, 1984, 2011 by Biblica, Inc. ®. Used by permission. All rights reserved worldwide.

Scripture quotations marked NLT are taken from Holy Bible, New Living Translation, copyright © 1996, 2004. 2015 by Tyndale House Foundation. Used by permission of Tyndale House Publishers, Inc., Carol Stream, Illinois 60188. All rights reserved.

All Scripture references marked NRSV are taken from the New Revised Standard Version Bible, copyright © 1989, the Division of Christian Education of the National Council of the Churches of Christ in the United States of America. Used by permission. All rights reserved.

TABLE OF CONTENTS

Thank You(s)………………………………………………………..	*page 4*
About the Author………………………………………………..	*page 6*
Reader's Dedication…………………………………………….	*page 7*
Fruit of the Spirit Hymns………………………………………	*page 8*
Suggested Daily Guide………………………………………….	*page 9*
Fruits of the Spirit Chart………………………………………..	*page 10*
Scripture Songs & Prayers……………………………………..	*page 11*
POEM: *You Are A Gift*………………………………………..	*page 12*
God's Ten Commandments……………………………………..	*page 13*
Introduction………………………………………………………	*page 14*
#1 UNFORGIVENESS…………………………………………	*page 15*
What Is a True Christian?…………………………………..	*page 20*
#2 GUILT………………………………………………………..	*page 22*
What Is Forgiveness?……………………………………….	*page 27*
#3 DEPRESSION………………………………………………	*page 29*
The Overcomer………………………………………………	*page 34*
#4 ANGER………………………………………………………	*page 36*
What Is Repentance?……………………………………….	*page 41*
#5 SELF-HATE………………………………………………….	*page 43*
Are You Ready to Give Up?…………………………………	*page 48*
#6 SELFISHNESS……………………………………………..	*page 50*
What Are Sins of the Flesh?………………………………..	*page 55*
#7 ANXIETY……………………………………………………	*page 57*
Consequences of Unforgiveness……………………………	*page 62*
#8 PRIDE……………………………………………………….	*page 64*
The Power of Prayer………………………………………..	*page 69*
#9 REVENGE, HATE………………………………………….	*page 71*
Perfected Character…………………………………………	*page 76*
Prayer List, Answered Prayers, & Reflective Thoughts………	*page 78*
Earnest Prayers & Songs………………………………………..	*page 83*
Additional Resources……………………………………………..	*page 87*

ACKNOWLEDGEMENTS

- **CHIEF EDITORS:**
  Karí Hart
  Anna Chiarenza

- **COVER DESIGNER:**
  Ricky Brome II

- **BOOK TITLE:**
  Ricky Brome II

- **SPIRITUAL ADVISOR:**
  My Heavenly Father

Abundant Gratitude

I am extremely grateful to have in my life two special women of God. They have been encouraging, patient, insightful, and sacrificial during this emotional project. Phenomenal editors and counselors to me, especially when the challenges came through doubts and wanting to quit. May each reader be inspired by your influences in this empowering devotion!

Thank you so much to **Karí Hart.**
An extremely patient and committed childhood friend (sister). She is also an astonishing Special Education teacher. May God continue to use and bless you enormously, as you guide, educate, and sacrifice for your students daily. You have been an incredible blessing to me as we grew together in the Lord through this project.

Abundant thanks to **Anna Chiarenza.**
Devoted mom, homeschool educator, and medical missionary. She has been such a great blessing and special sister in Christ, as we encourage each other through our parenting journey. She is passionate about doing God's will through the gift of writing to further the gospel and health message.

"In keeping others out we are really imprisoning ourselves!"
~Anna Chiarenza

THANK YOU!

Special Thanks

A special thank you to my son, *Ricky Brome II*.

For the thought-provoking book title, cover design, and inserted words of wisdom throughout this devotion. Thanks as well as for the additional insights shared regarding content, songs, and layout.

*Ricky, this book is **specially dedicated** to you, an extraordinary messenger for Christ! He has gifted you with so much: A God-given public speaker, excellent counselor, musician, singer, and a humble servant! I pray this book helps to empower your Christian walk and for you to stay faithful to "The End."*

Remember to always unapologetically follow your heavenly Father's footsteps all the days of your life …

I love you enormously, my son!
~Luke 12:48

Unique Surprise!

To my patient and loving husband, *Rob Shepherd*.

Thank you for your patience and support throughout our marriage. God has innumerable blessings in store for your life. Continue to walk closely with Him and listen diligently for His voice.

I wanted this devotion to be a surprise for you, and yes, it sure was difficult trying to pull it off. Writing on the side while trying to find time to complete my daily "Honey-do list." ☺

So Honey … "**SURPRISE!!!**"

Thank you for being an amazing father, a godly husband, and a loyal and passionate man of God. I pray this devotional is encouraging to your heart.

I Love You!

the AUTHOR

An Imperfect Servant of Christ!

I am unworthy and undeserving of grace, but thank God, He has found me worthy of His abundant grace. I am a grateful mother and wife, finally ready and willing to do the Savior's will. I have resisted God's calling for many years. But at last, I have accepted the calling to give a message of hope to those who are hurting. I am saddened that I have waited so long to listen to God's voice and have missed the mark for so many years. I was too wrapped up in my own issues of life, as a result, I lost out on helping those who were suffering in silence, but God is merciful. Do not create your own imprisonment of the mind; this does not bring glory to the Father. **We must learn to die to self, to fully remove selfishness!**

Our world is hurting and many are lost in need of a Savior. Why should the world continue to suffer when God has placed each of us here to be of service to the other? God is calling us to be a community of love and hope, to walk as He walked in fellowship. *"Father, give us a zeal to share Your word with those we come in contact with."* **~Corrine Brown**

HOW TO PROCEED:

> - First, commit to your daily devotions for the next thirty days, with deep earnest prayers, songs, and scriptures. I have included a hymn page and scripture song page (links included), to go with each devotional topic.
> - Secondly, make your worship a joyous occasion, not just a daily checklist. Christ desires an intimate relationship with you and to spend quality time together each day.
> - Finally, personalize your daily worship; you will then begin to experience a change, an actual connection with the Savior. You cannot get to know Christ deeply with one foot in the world and one in the church. Life is too painful and traumatic this way, the world has nothing to give but momentary enjoyments. You must desire to get to the point in your walk where the enemy can no longer use you for his glory. As my husband likes to say, *"When we do devil activities, we get devil results."* **~Rob Shepherd**

I pray this devotional will be a blessing to you as it has been for me. I tearfully write to you, as I too, have grown closer to my Savior through this journey. If no one else, this book has touched my heart, revealed my pride, and brought me humbly before the throne of God.

This might be a painful and emotional journey for you to finally surrender your will, but Christ is ready to walk hand in hand with you. Thank You Father for Your compassionate mercy on Your flock! So, get lost in the pages with Christ, and you too, will obtain that abundant blessing you deserve. **I am praying for you!**

**JOIN THE JOURNEY:*

READER'S PRAYER OF DEDICATION

To every heart reading these words. Tremendous blessings upon your life! Desiring a personal relationship with God is what will transform your life and fulfill all your emptiness. Many times you may feel alone in your sufferings, but you aren't. Reach out to someone for support and you will find there are others going through similar challenges and are suffering alone. However, during your difficulties, consider how God is allowing your situation to be used for His glory. Oftentimes, His glory is seen through you during the development of your character. Character change is essential to enter into the heavenly kingdom! When you walk closely with your Savior, everything else seems bearable; this is due to you fully trusting and relying upon His wisdom and direction for your life.

The character you need to attain must reflect the fruit of the spirit: **Christ's character**. So, even when people toss you to the side, God is always there with His abundant love, ready to help you blossom and be made new. You cannot attain Joy without Peace, Faith without Patience, Kindness without Goodness, nor Self-control without Humility… but most of all, you cannot have any of these without **Love!**

Your obedience and faith is what's most valuable to God. We are all **nothing**, but Christ has chosen **nothing** to do something (that's you and me), and little is much when God is in it. Micah 6:8, author's paraphrase, *"God has showed you what is good, and what He requires of you, to do justly and love with mercy and to walk humbly with our God."* Your Savior has chosen you to share His gospel to a dying world.

MAN OF GOD

To a man of God, ready to fulfill God's mission. You have been created for greatness and purpose. May God help you to be diligent in your daily devotions, drawing you closer to Him.

Your path of salvation is not just for you, it's for those around you, who you will be influencing. You may have heard of Christ or believe in Him, but there is a difference when you experience Him.

Lord, lead this man of God, to Your righteous ways. Forgive him and find him worthy to enter into Your eternal kingdom!

WOMAN OF GOD

To a woman of God, longing to do God's will. Help her to be spiritually transformed and inspired to help those who are suffering around her. Being of service to others is not just a blessing for others, but also for her.

Lord, use her, according to Your will, as she listens daily for Your instructions. Give her peace, give her strength, to deny the evils of this lost world.

Speak to her heart, O Lord, give her Your Holy Word. Rejoicing as You proudly claim her as a child of Your kingdom!

FRUITS OF THE SPIRIT HYMNS

#1 LOVE (Unforgiveness)............... *Forgive Our Sins, As We Forgive*

#2 JOY (Guilt).. *As Water to the Thirsty*

#3 PEACE (Depression).......................... *Will Your Anchor Hold?*

#4 PATIENCE (Anger)...................... *Live Out Thy Life Within Me*

#5 KINDNESS (Self-hate)...................................... *Give Me Jesus*

#6 GOODNESS (Selfish)..................... *Take My Life and Let It Be*

#7 FAITH (Anxiety).. *Be Still, My Soul*

#8 HUMBLE (Pride)................................. *The Savior is Waiting*

#9 SELF-CONTROL (Revenge)......... *O, For a Closer Walk With God*

WORTHY............................. *This Is My Father's World*
TRIALS........................ *I Want Jesus to Walk With Me*
GLIMPE OF HOPE................................ *Rock of Ages*
REPENTANCE............................. *Draw Me Nearer*
FULL SURRENDER........................... *Jesus, I Come*
VICTORY SHOUT................ *O, When Shall I See Jesus*
REPENTANCE.......... *Is This the Day of New Beginnings*
DIFFICULTIES: HOLD ON......... *The Old Rugged Cross*

~I PRAY THESE SONGS ARE A BLESSING TO YOUR SOUL, AS THEY ARE TO MINE!
https://www.youtube.com/watch?v=izm0sSd4VFc

Suggested Daily Guide

10 Natural Health Remedies

There are **10 natural remedies** that God has given us to maintain a healthy mind and body, so we may glorify Him. We will cover these in 3 categories.
"To jumpstart my day I begin with what I like to call the 3 W's: Worship, Workout, and Work!" ~**Rob Shepherd**

1. WORSHIP

1. **Daily devotion:** Early morning is best — the world is quieter, no interruptions, and you can hear God's voice more clearly. **#1-2 YIELD YOUR WILL, GRATITUDE!**
2. **Read 1 page per day:** Memorize and meditate on the included scriptures. There are a lot of details here, so reflect and deliberate on each story, question, prayer, and journal your thought. A prayer list and answered prayers is included at the end of the devotional, for daily use. Also, there are scripture song links for you to enjoy! **#3 TRUSTING GOD!**
3. **Scripture reading:** Replace your name in each verse. This helps you to experience a deeper meaning, i.e. James 4:17 KJV, *"To your name who knoweth to do good, and doeth it not, to your name it is sin."* This will help you to embark on a personalized journey.

2. WORKOUT

1. **Cardio, gym, or nature:** Nature is the best remedy, driving to a park and just listening the birds, watching the squirrels, or looking at the water. We feel God's love and hear His voice more. When we complete this category we are able to accomplish four of the eight remedies daily: **#4–7 EXERCISE, FRESH AIR, SUNSHINE, WATER!**
2. **Wholesome breakfast after:** Includes fruits, nuts, and grains. Try to eat foods from the ground, these are unprocessed and God's natural nutrients. **#8 NUTRITION!**

3. WORK

1. **Positive attitude:** Carry an uplifting attitude throughout the day; this is contagious. Find a way to bless someone, even if it's helping them to smile.
Focus on Christ in your frustrations, and stay humble!
2. **Medium lunch:** Your lunch should be medium-sized; if hungry later, a light dinner. No late-night eating: after 7 p.m. **#9 SELF-CONTROL!**
3. **Proper sleep:** Aim to sleep by 10 p.m. each night. It's said when we sleep before midnight, we get double the rest. At 10 p.m. we would get four hours of rest by midnight instead of only two hours. Remove all technology devices from your room, to reduce radiation. Sleep also helps to heal the body and reduce weight gain. **#10 REST!**

Salvation is a Gift, Not a Reward!

Fruits of the Holy Spirit

ATTAINED	LACKING
#1 LOVE: Compassionate to those around you, especially your enemies. A Christ-like character needed to teach and reach the world.	**LACK of Love:** Compassionate only to those who please you; harsh feelings or hate for your enemies. A misrepresentation of Christ's character.
#2 JOY: Bringing cheerfulness and zeal to those you encounter. Having a light of Christ radiating from you to share with the world.	**LACK of Joy:** Bringing gloom and darkness to yourself and others around you. Showing only situational happiness in things.
#3 PEACE: Stability and calmness in your mind and body. Trusting and relying on God for peace, even during your trials.	**LACK of Peace:** Causing strife and conflict with others; frequently experiencing spiritual battles; love of gossip; holding on to a victim mentality.
#4 PATIENCE: Endurance with no murmuring and misery; slow to speak; being content.	**LACK of Patience:** Persistent whining and complaining, even during simple task; an unpleasant character.
#5 KINDNESS: Cheerful and willing to do for others, even if inconvenienced. Forgiving and patient with self.	**LACK of Kindness:** Mean-spirited; looking out for self; unpleasant to be around; unfriendly; unforgiving.
#6 GOODNESS: Having a pleasant demeanor; thoughtful and helpful at home and in the community.	**LACK of Goodness:** Unsympathetic to others; puts self first or superficially puts others first (for show).
#7 FAITHFUL: Experiencing a cherished walk with God. A doer of His word, not just a hearer; trustworthy.	**LACK of Faith:** Wavering in Christ; unable to be consistent; doubtful: anxious; unreliable; unfulfilled.
#8 HUMBLE: Merciful and gracious; the ability to influence a situation with calmness and wisdom.	**LACK of Humility:** Uncontrollable; prideful; untactful; haughty and unresponsive to wisdom; know it all.
#9 SELF-CONTROL: Having the mind of Christ; shunning all addictive behaviors: appetite, lust, and outbursts; power given to overcome temptation.	**LACK of Self-control:** Giving in to all passions: food, impulses, emotions; unable to resist the darkness of sin thus giving in to temptations.

SCRIPTURE SONGS AND PRAYERS

#1 LOVE..*Luke 17:3–6*
SCRIPTURE SONG: (Unforgiveness) *Isaiah 55:6–9*
https://www.youtube.com/watch?v=V2asZ15Xkdk

#2 JOY..*Jeremiah 29:11–13*
SCRIPTURE SONG: (Guilt) *Proverbs 17:22*
https://www.youtube.com/watch?v=nAPaCvXoz54

#3 PEACE..*Psalm 116:1–2*
SCRIPTURE SONG: (Depression) *Isaiah 41: 9–10, 13, 18*
https://www.youtube.com/watch?v=73QCDag9dYY

#4 PATIENCE...*James 1:2–8, 26*
SCRIPTURE SONG: (Anger) *James 1:2–4*
https://www.youtube.com/watch?v=924bcgoVWdE

#5 KINDNESS..*Psalm 40*
SCRIPTURE SONG: (Self-hate) *Psalm 40:1–3, 5, 16*
https://www.youtube.com/watch?v=N34vdV5hAi4

#6 GOODNESS..*Philippians 2*
SCRIPTURE SONG: (Selfish) *Philippians 2:3–4*
https://www.youtube.com/watch?v=eldh_gtwYyQ

#7 FAITH..*Psalm 27*
SCRIPTURE SONG: (Anxiety) *Psalm 27:1, 3–4, 7, 10, 14*
https://www.youtube.com/watch?v=AWCr-hs8Ujk

#8 HUMBLE...*James 4*
SCRIPTURE SONG: (Pride) *James 4:7–10*
https://www.youtube.com/watch?v=UnF69Rq1Bno

#9 SELF-CONTROL..*James 1:19–22*
SCRIPTURE SONG: (Revenge) *Psalm 139:23–24*
https://www.youtube.com/watch?v=SWUQ5vVPXIM

~MY PRAYER FOR YOU~

May your soul be at peace in the laws of our heavenly Father, as a loyal and true follower. There is nothing in this world more precious. May you find your true purpose and fulfillment in Him!

https://www.youtube.com/watch?v=KKtG7Z5DubU

POEM

You Are A Gift!

Fruits of the Spirit

God's Spirit makes us loving, happy, peaceful, patient, kind, good, faithful, gentle, and self-controlled. There is no law against behaving in any of these ways.
Galatians 5:22–23

A Gift for God!

You have been molded by God. A peculiar person in His Royal Priesthood. He has formed and designed every inch of you, demonstrating the tender love and care He has just for you. Imagine the heavenly discussion that was had; what would make you unique, what would set you apart and the impact you would leave upon others and the world.

It is your responsibility to yourself and to those around you to let patience, kindness, goodness, peace, faith, joy, love, humility, and self-control become a part of your very being. Only then will things that are pure, lovely, and of good report be your experience. **Contemplate:** *what is your purpose in Christ's mission?*

Date Accomplished:

Begin: 1ˢᵗ FRUIT
Date:_____

LOVE that God has bestowed upon us, a light entrusted to us to shine to the world.

Middle: 5ᵗʰ FRUIT
Date:_____

KINDNESS to do good and bring a blessing to a broken world, through Christ's character.

End: 9ᵗʰ FRUIT
Date:_____

SELF-CONTROL with the help of the Holy Spirit, we can attain. Attain moderation in the good things and avoidance of bad habits, thoughts, and behaviors.

GOD'S Ten Commandments

Exodus 20:1–17 KJV

¹ And God spake all these words, saying,

² I *am* the Lord thy God, which have brought thee out of the land of Egypt, out of the house of bondage.

³ Thou shalt have no other gods before me. **#1**

⁴ Thou shalt not make unto thee any graven image, or any likeness *of any thing* that *is* in heaven above, or that *is* in the earth beneath, or that *is* in the water under the earth: **#2**

⁵ Thou shalt not bow down thyself to them, nor serve them: for I the Lord thy God *am* a jealous God, visiting the iniquity of the fathers upon the children unto the third and fourth *generation* of them that hate me;

⁶ And shewing mercy unto thousands of them that love me, and keep my commandments.

⁷ Thou shalt not take the name of the Lord thy God in vain; for the Lord will not hold him guiltless that taketh his name in vain. **#3**

⁸ Remember the sabbath day, to keep it holy. **#4**

⁹ Six days shalt thou labour, and do all thy work:

¹⁰ But the seventh day *is* the sabbath of the Lord thy God: *in it* thou shalt not do any work, thou, nor thy son, nor thy daughter, thy manservant, nor thy maidservant, nor thy cattle, nor thy stranger that *is* within thy gates:

¹¹ For *in* six days the Lord made heaven and earth, the sea, and all that in them *is*, and rested the seventh day: wherefore the Lord blessed the sabbath day, and hallowed it.

¹² Honour thy father and thy mother: that thy days may be long upon the land which the Lord thy God giveth thee. **#5**

¹³ Thou shalt not kill. **#6**

¹⁴ Thou shalt not commit adultery. **#7**

¹⁵ Thou shalt not steal. **#8**

¹⁶ Thou shalt not bear false witness against thy neighbour. **#9**

¹⁷ Thou shalt not covet thy neighbour's house, thou shalt not covet thy neighbour's wife, nor his manservant, nor his maidservant, nor his ox, nor his ass, nor any thing that is thy neighbour's. **#10**

CHOOSE TODAY WHO YOU WILL SERVE?

- ○ Your Glorious and Loving Heavenly Father!
- ○ The Enemy and Father of Deception and Lies!

INTRODUCTION

So, what does God have in store for your life?

Have you considered if Earth is your final home or is there a more marvelous life hereafter? Which life are you striving for, the earthly or the heavenly?

Here Are A Few Questions To Consider:

How is your character right now? Has it been perfected? Have you been a good example for Christ? How about the character of others in the church? Have they shown a noble example of Christ's love or of a worldly unconverted heart? Have you allowed these unconverted hearts to separate you from your intimacy with Christ?

I can speak from experience, and testify to that. I walked away from Christ in my youth. It felt so justified, because I had bad examples of Christ. But what I did was rob Christ of my obedience and the love He deserved.

Unfortunately, there are many situations of ungodly people in the church, and this is Satan's deception to pull Christ's children out of the church. The spirit of **doubt** sets in saying, *"Well, if church folks are this way and claim to know Christ, I don't want to be here. I'm better off in the world."*

We must remember we are all sinful, looking for Christ to help change our hearts so that we can wear His character. Many attend church but do not dig daily for a deeper connection, thus they fail the necessary heart conversion. *"Too many people allow others to steal their joy in a lot of ways."* ~**Rob Shepherd**

But, like Christ did for me, He can also do for you. He gave me hope, and I returned to Him.

REMEMBER, *SIN SEPARATES* YOU FROM GOD!

REFLECTING ON A SITUATION:

I remember when a high-positioned person in my church approached me, stating that he wanted to marry me if anything ever happened to his wife (i.e. died). **I WAS SICKENED!!!**
I felt so dirty, cheap, and offended. But most of all, his wife didn't have a godly husband who was concerned about helping each other get to heaven. His commitment was only for his fleshly desires.

"In order for a sinner to get help from God, they must first be convicted of their sins." ~**Corrine Brown**
Many Christians believe they will make it to heaven just because they believe in Christ, but they have totally deceived themselves. Can we enter God's righteous presence in heaven in such a sinful state? We *must* surrender and repent, relying only on Christ for strength to overcome our daily sinful desires.
WE MUST DIE TO SELF!

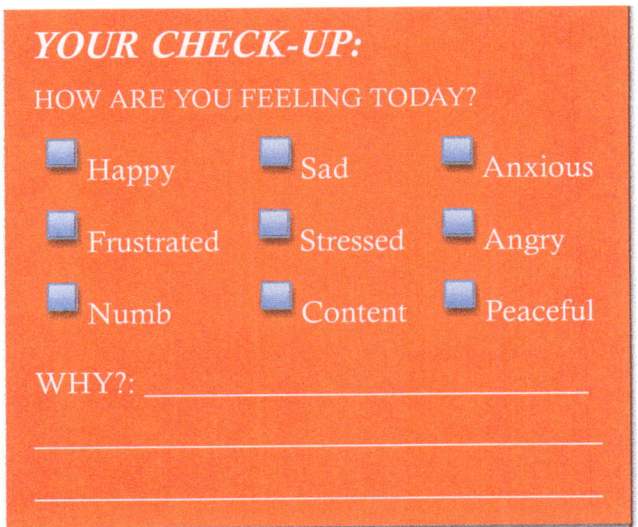

SYMPTOMS:
bitterness, hurt, anger, malice, rage, impatience, blaming, low self-esteem, victim mentality, hate

YOUR CHECK-UP:
HOW ARE YOU FEELING TODAY?

☐ Happy   ☐ Sad   ☐ Anxious
☐ Frustrated   ☐ Stressed   ☐ Angry
☐ Numb   ☐ Content   ☐ Peaceful

WHY?: _____
_____
_____

Did You Know?

Unforgiveness originates from a series of unfortunate circumstances, here are just a few:

Having childhood trauma (neglect, verbal, sexual, or physical abuse)

Being belittled in front of others

Feeling unloved or rejected

Being bullied

Blaming yourself for poor decisions

Being assaulted or raped

Blaming God for negative outcomes

An unfaithful partner

Feeling offended, and the list goes on…

UNFORGIVENESS

So, what's preventing you from forgiving?

Are you giving your best, feeling success financially and healthwise, as well as being emotionally stable? Or are you pretending to the world and dying inside?

What if I told you you're only fooling yourself? You might feel like you have it all under control, but unforgiveness is actually controlling your thoughts, your heart, your actions, and your life. How long will you continue living this way, but not really living at all? Simply getting by or maybe appearing successful, but feeling unlovable, unfulfilled, and unhappy. I don't think I need to tell you this, but this is no way to exist.
You cannot live your life to the fullest this way!

You might be bitter about something in your past, a bad marriage, difficult co-parenting, an unloving parent, how about even an adult that violated your trust as a child. You're thinking, they wronged me and these are justifiable reasons for you not to ever forgive, but I'm here to tell you, you're the only one in the situation missing out. Choosing to live in the prison of mental bondage. I don't want this for you. **It's too exhausting!**

The limited life you are living today is a choice. Life has so much more to offer you. God is simply waiting on you to let go. Forgiveness breaks the power of sin and creates healing for you. **This brings you an unimaginable peace.**

Holding On Tight!

Is unforgiveness keeping you on the edge of the cliff? I know forgiveness can be challenging, but this is necessary for your peace, joy, and overall health. You also cannot fully love with an unforgiving heart; you are only deceiving yourself.

I remember dating and being in a relationship that I thought was almost perfect. I didn't want to hear any negative comments from my family or friends; I was so in love. A few months later, I remember getting my first hit in the face. Of course, we all know what comes next: "I'm so sorry, it won't happen again," over and over. But these were only empty promises. I finally wised up after the fourth altercation that ended with me unconscious on the floor. I blacked out, as he strangled me in rage.

For many years, I was angry, bitter, regretful, hurt, and humiliated. I held on to this unforgiveness throughout my life. Walking daily under a dark cloud without realizing it had become the new me. I had temporary happiness at times, but no true joy and no real peace. Simply feeling alone and imprisoned inside my own mind. **Have you experienced this?**

Only God Can Heal!

Unforgiveness robbed me of my joy, love, potential in life, and ultimately my purpose for Christ. Unforgiveness is poison to your mind and spirit, as well as those you come in contact with. Remember, forgiveness is not for the "offender" but for the "wounded." There were so many suffering I could have helped, if only I had removed **self** sooner to be a blessing to them.

You might have experienced molestation by a family member, abandonment, had neglectful parents, betrayal in a relationship, a nasty boss, wrongfully imprisoned, cancer, the loss of a child (emotionally), or angry about the death of a loved one. However, holding on to this unforgiveness only injures the heart, takes your joy, and steals away your ordained purpose and **love** for others.

When you choose not to forgive, you spend more time with your offender than you realize. Allowing them to control your emotions: anger, bitterness, revengeful thoughts, and a constant unfulfillment. Only the power of the Holy Spirit gives you the desire to forgive. Ask for this. Contemplate how God has forgiven you **abundantly** when you have neglected, rejected, or hurt Him. Reflecting on how He has treated you hopefully motivates you to forgive those you deem unworthy of your mercy.

Conditional or Unconditional?

Did you know the bitterness you harbor in your heart even affects the way you do things for God? For example, it will affect how you do things for God, for yourself, at church, at your school, in your relationships, and so on. If you are being truthful, you will realize the love you say you have for others is purely conditional or superficial. When someone does something to offend you, your expression of love may diminish, turning into anger, selfishness, malice, or negative thoughts. **But, is this Christ's method?** With a specific prayer each day, consecrate your life and heart to the Lord; without this you will **never** overcome.

Let us remember the compassion of **Steven** in Acts 7:59–60. It shows us how we must remove self even when we are victims because our real reward is eternity in heaven with our Savior. Christ definitely sympathizes with those who have been taken advantage of. However, He does not want us to stay trapped in the past, reliving our trauma. This only leaves us feeling bitter, empty, and unable to forgive ourselves and others. God desires for us to heal, so we can be a joyful, peaceful light, to this corrupt world, eager to do His will. Steven, a faithful follower of Christ, had the heart of his Savior, even upon death. **How about you?**

Use your experiences to become a restored servant, to help those that may be in similar situations to begin their healing.

Are You Separated?

Do not allow unforgiveness to separate you from God. You must beg and plead with the Lord for the deliverance of any dark spirits; these are not of His character.

Plead for Him to help you not to be a "surface" Christian, but a converted follower. Imagine how this behavior must hurt Christ? Your prayer ought to be, "Lord, help me not to be a Christian only on the outside for others to see and a willful sinner on the inside. Remember, God already knows your heart. Begin pleading with your heavenly Father for help. Psalm 118:8 tells us, don't look to man first. He wants us to seek Him persistently first.

Release your pains, trust God, forgive as He has forgiven you even when you have offended Him, and enjoy the **joys of forgiveness.** Consider this: your trials are a testimony of **God's love**. He will take you through, while molding you for your eternal destination with Him. Christ has already sacrificed everything for you. Can you now sacrifice everything for Him?

What is a Christian?

1. Pleasant or mean?
2. Cheerful or gloomy?
3. Kind or annoyed?
4. Thoughtful or selfish?
5. Compassionate or unforgiving?
6. Lives in darkness or in light?
7. Converted outside (surface) or inside (the heart)?

LOVE   LOVE   LOVE

We live in an imperfect world, and sadly, this is the consequence of sin. All will experience pain, hurt, and challenges throughout their lives, just as Christ did for you. But could you be holding on to more than just the burdens of unforgiveness? Consider this: you could be in violation of God's laws? Perhaps you're saying, no, that's not possible. I love and honor Him each day. So let's dig a little deeper then. Many times when we hold on to something for so long, especially if its harmful for us, we aren't aware or it's become addictive for us. So much so, we are loving and treasuring it more than God. Could unforgiveness be your new god? Think about that, how long has it been?

You might be experiencing some resistance right now, because it is difficult to admit we love anything more than our compassionate Savior. However, this is the first commandment given to us, to have no other gods before Him, **Exodus 20:3.** If we are spending more time glorifying our hurts, we have an idol. We have replaced the one true God with a false god called justified unforgiveness or offenses. Deep down inside you know you're only hurting yourself.

FORGIVE AND BE SET FREE!

FROM GOD: FORGIVE, AS I WILL NOT GIVE UP ON YOU!

Christ, Our Example ...

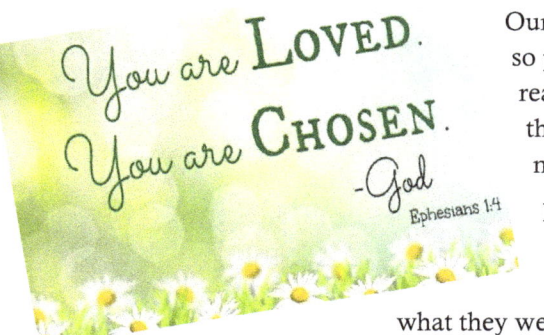

Our duty to Christ is to be a powerful witness for Him, so people can view God in a positive light! Do you realize how hard we are on people that do not know the light of Christ? Think about the fact that they do not know the dark spirits that control them?

Even Christ in His sacrifice at the cross (Luke 23:32–34), while being continually belittled, asked His Father to forgive them, because they knew not what they were doing. They wore a spirit of darkness that veiled their eyes and blinded them of their sins. So if Christ, our example, was able to forgive His betrayers in the very act, can we not also forgive those who have hurt us? Of course, we can, but only with Christ. We must ask for His help! Forgive as the Lord continues to forgive your daily offenses. Then receive His peace and **love** in your heart today. **Heal your mind and body!**

AFTER TIME WITH CHRIST:

HOW DO YOU FEEL?

☐ Happy   ☐ Sad   ☐ Anxious

☐ Frustrated   ☐ Stressed   ☐ Angry

☐ Numb   ☐ Content   ☐ Peaceful

COMMENT: _____
_____
_____

Who Made The Sacrifice?

The ultimate sacrifice has already been done for you, do not allow it to be in vain. They say forgiveness is a gift you give yourself, but I say, forgiveness is God's greatest **Gift** to you. **So take it!**

"Let this mind be in you, which was also in Christ Jesus: Who, being in the form of God, thought it not robbery to be equal with God: But made himself of no reputation, and took upon him the form of a servant, and was made in the likeness of men... he humbled himself, and became obedient unto death, even the death of the cross." Philippians 2:5-8

HUMBLE YOURSELF & ACCEPT THE GIFT OF FORGIVENESS!

Your Prayer

_____
_____
_____, AMEN!

WHAT IS A TRUE CHRISTIAN?

Many believe that being a Christian simply means believing God exists. Consider this. Satan also believes that God exists, so this is not enough. Being a true follower is significantly deeper than that. God is love. If you are not displaying love to others, then you are not a true Christian. Do not allow yourself to be deceived and find out at Christ's return that you made it to the wrong side, the enemy's side. How devastating this will be for any of us!

"Christianity begins in the heart; it's not an outward show." ~**Corrine Brown**

It's one thing to **believe about** Christ, but another thing to **believe in** Christ. John 14:12 KJV tells us, "He that believeth on me, the works that I do shall he do also; and greater works than these shall he do; because I go unto my Father." *A true Christian strives to follow daily in the footsteps of their Savior.*

As a true Christian, your words must demonstrate that your mind is centered on Christ and that your life is completely surrendered to do His will. Here is the bottom line. With a true conversion, your thoughts, words, and behavior will match that of Christ's. Reflecting kindness, meekness, and honesty. As a result, Christ will remove impatience, hate, pride, gossip, and the list goes on... *Surrender today your will to Him!*

ARE YOU A TRUE CHRISTIAN?

Here are a few signs of a true Christian:

- You have love and compassion for others as Christ did while He was here in His earthly ministry. You have a desire to help those in need.

- You long for a thoughtful moment each day, seeking to learn more about your Savior and His sacrifice.

- You've had a personal encounter, and now your joy is found in Christ. (Not others or things)

- You strive daily to follow in the footsteps of your Savior because love abounds for Him.

- You honor and obey the commandments of God because of the deep intimate love you have with Him.

- You commune daily through prayer and petition on others' behalf. (Phil 4:6–7)

- You display a spirit of peace and gratitude.

JOURNAL THOUGHTS

GUILT

A merry heart doeth good like a medicine:
but a broken spirit drieth the bones.
Proverbs 17:22

SYMPTOMS:
distrust, anxiety, anger, grief, shame, unforgiving, embarrassment, discontentment, illness, self-hate,

YOUR CHECK-UP:

HOW ARE YOU FEELING TODAY?

☐ Happy ☐ Sad ☐ Anxious

☐ Frustrated ☐ Stressed ☐ Angry

☐ Numb ☐ Content ☐ Peaceful

WHY?: _____
_____
_____

LET IT GO!

Why are you walking daily down the road of shame? Do you believe there is something terrible you cannot be forgiven of? You have continued to live in this entrapment for months, years, and even decades!

Do you know guilt eats away at the heart, causing sickness and disease? Are you still blaming yourself for the bad choices in your past? Are you finding it hard to trust others because you don't trust yourself? Are you still blaming someone for hurting you? Have you blamed yourself for hurting someone in the past? Are you trying to figure out why it's so difficult to forgive yourself? **I'll tell you the secret.** You're simply trying to do it all on your own. There is nothing good we can do for ourselves; our efforts are in vain without Christ's help.

GUILT

The Silent Thief …

Do you truly understand the love the Christ has for you? He has gifted you with a world so beautiful. If you are unable to see this, let's talk about why!

When we are in bondage, many times we are unaware and unable to see the daily **love notes,** God leaves for us:
The immaculate skies, chirping birds, majestic waterfalls, vibrant sunshine, the blessings of good health, positive friendships, or even a warm smile.

Guilt steals your joy from within and prevents you from experiencing true joy, or to even give God the glory He deserves. You must lay all your guilt at the feet of your Savior, earnestly confess and repent, develop a spirit of praise, which blossoms into a spirit of gratitude. God accepts your broken spirit and contrite heart, offers you pardon, and welcomes you into His family. You must learn to believe and accept His forgiveness, and forgive yourself.

Let us not dishonor God by doubting His forgiveness and love for us.

The **Guilt** of King David

Let's recall one of **King David's** weak moments. He desired a married woman, pursued relations with her, and she became pregnant. **So what do you think his next move was?** He plotted to kill her husband to cover up his sins, by sending him out into battle to die.
Mission Accomplished!

However, this act tormented David continually. Guilt eats away at your vital forces and weighs you down as if you are carrying an invisible elephant on your back.

Psalm 51:1–15 says King David asked God to have mercy upon him, to hide his face from his sins, to not cast him away from the presence of God, and to restore the joy of his salvation. **Why did David do this with such a repentant spirit?** Without this spirit, you will persistently remain imprisoned by the enemy's *bondage of guilty accusations.*

The Hidden Cause

Did you know there are times things may feel good but it doesn't mean they're good for us. For example: a tasty donut, or a recipe for rice that has sugar added to it. That sugar will eventually impact your life down the road. Well how about in the case of gossip? This might feel good, in a group or one on one, but did you know there are dangers associated in gossiping, whether the offender or the victim?

Gossiping, factual or not, does not glorify the Savior. Scripture tells us in Philippians 2:3, *"Let nothing be done through strife or vain glory; but in lowliness of mind let each esteem other better than themselves."*

Gossip also takes the attention off self and helps us to feel better about ourselves short-term, but this unknowingly affects our mental state in the long-term. Guilt, criticism, and unfulfillment begin to rule your life, not knowing the root cause is gossip.

Could we also be in defilement of the Ten Commandments, number nine? Are we bearing false witness against our neighbor? Are you defiling that person's character so you may shine instead? Imagine how this behavior must hurt Christ. This is the result of a surface Christian. Yield to Him for help, so you're no longer a "surface" Christian, but a converted follower of His. Your prayer ought to be, "Lord, help me not to be only a Christian on the outside for others to see, while being a willful sinner on the inside." You are only deceiving yourself.

You must ask for deliverance from gossip, as this sin is even seen in the church at times. It does not bring unity, only strife and division. This sin is crippling to your Christian walk, and you are unable to achieve intimacy with Christ. If someone brings it to you, whether the facts are correct or not, change the subject, or say to them, let's pray for this person, or if possible, ask how can we be a blessing to that person. This slows or stops negative people inside and outside the church from coming to you. They will see that you stand for something better, a higher calling for Christ. I would like to remind you also, that gossip will keep you out of the gates of heaven. But there is nothing so

shameful in your life that God is not willing to clean you of. Do not let this addictive behavior separate you from the eternal blessings God has prepared just for you in glory.

Without full surrender and obedience, you can never show up and shine for Christ, and you will not find the path of purpose He has written on your life. Humble yourself (acknowledge and admit), confess (ask for forgiveness), and repent (change your ways to please God). He will heal you from the struggle of guilt and shame of gossip.

Your Secret Ingredient!

Life might be tough at times, but the **Joyful** reward you receive after you've gone through the fire, the trials, and the tough times while leaning on Christ is indescribable.

"Being happy truly gives us health benefits. If you take time to look at the far-reaching effects of these benefits, you would see that happiness is just an overall incredible life-extender that also helps us to be more productive in life." ~**Ricky Brome II**

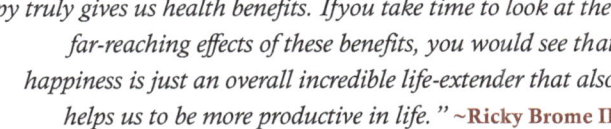

Are you allowing life to beat you down, steal your joy, or even bring on illness? That is such an empty experience in this world. Lean on Christ more. You have such an amazing story ahead of you. He is listening for your voice, He is longing for an intimacy with you.

Try Gratitude; a life of Gratefulness is a life of Abundance!

Psalm 100:4-5 tells us, "Enter into his gates with thanksgiving, and into his courts with praise: be thankful unto him, and bless his name." Our first step is to remove ourselves, then our guilt. Be thankful and praise the Lord's name instead, his mercies will be bestowed upon us greatly. It is time to forgive self.

WHICH LIFE DO YOU CHOOSE?

SYMPTOMS OF JOY:	SYMPTOMS OF GUILT:
❖ Peace	❖ Anxiety
❖ Kindness	❖ Self Doubt
❖ Gratitude	❖ Distrust
❖ Healthy relationships	❖ Discomfort
❖ Forgiving	❖ Remorse
❖ Satisfaction	❖ Low self-esteem
❖ Enjoyment	❖ Self-loathing
❖ Integrity	❖ Negative thoughts
❖ Feeling accomplished	❖ Overreactive
❖ Choose to let go of negative thoughts	❖ Sensitive

JOY

FROM GOD: GIVE ME YOUR BURDENS, I WILL MAKE THEM LIGHT!

Christ, Our Example …

Christ deserves your **joy**. If you are not joyous, you will become sick. Give God the praises He deserves and reflect His character each day. This allows others to see His light through you and removes the enemy's influence over your life. Christ gives us the recipe for J.O.Y; (J)esus first, (O)thers second, and then (Y)ourself. Wake up each morning thankful and say, "Lord, I surrender, please develop my character today. Help me to walk in Your footsteps to give You the glory." Christ gives us an example of how He relied upon His Father daily in John 15:10–11. **Please read.**

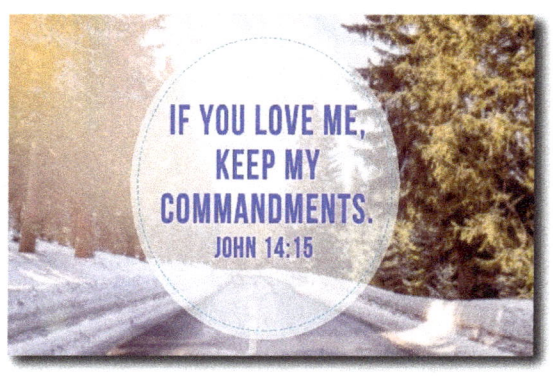

There is no greater satisfaction, no greater joy than when you choose to obey God's commandments. This is how you truly show your love for Him through willful obedience. Then experiencing the fullness of genuine joy, He remains in you and in your character. Do not let the enemy keep you hostage; **you deserve so much more** than what he's offering. Christ is your only hope!

AFTER TIME WITH CHRIST:

HOW DO YOU FEEL?

- ☐ Happy
- ☐ Sad
- ☐ Anxious
- ☐ Frustrated
- ☐ Stressed
- ☐ Angry
- ☐ Numb
- ☐ Content
- ☐ Peaceful

COMMENT: _____
_____
_____

Your Prayer

_____
_____
_____
_____
_____
_____
_____
_____
_____
_____
_____
_____
_____
_____
_____, AMEN!

WHAT IS FORGIVENESS?

The story in Matthew 18:21–35 gives us a great contrast of true forgiveness verses unforgiveness. Please read before continuing. After being forgiven by his master for an exuberant debt, this same vengeful servant was unable to forgive his fellow brother for a minuscule debt. This is the perfect replica for many Christian lives today: holding a grudge, pretending to love, and cherishing our unforgiveness. Are you following the Master's example of true forgiveness, or are you still clinging to your bitterness as a treasured gift? *"Remember, forgiveness is a healing process that benefits us more than it benefits anyone else."* **~Ricky Brome II**

HOW DOES UNFORGIVENESS IMPACT YOUR LIFE?

1. THERE ARE NEGATIVE IMPACTS ON YOUR HEALTH

Many diseases that exist today are due to the negative emotions we harbor inside; anger, resentment, hurt, etc. These diseases range from: depression, heart disease, ulcers, cancers, anxiety, addictions, to migraines, etc. *Your body is simply sympathizing with the mind.*

2. IT POISONS YOUR CHARACTER

Unforgiveness poisons our heart, mind, and mouth. When others are around you, they experience the bitterness and wrath that is deep within your heart. The anger you had from being wronged might have been justified, but forgiveness was the next step, and you refused. **Don't be discouraged—there is hope!** Remember, forgiveness is for you, not the offender. Unforgiveness blocks your ability to heal your emotional wounds and keeps your mind imprisoned. Since you have allowed it to grow into an enormous monster, now you have become that monster! Everyone dreads being around you due to your destructive communication patterns. So, how long will you live this way? **Are you ready to forgive?**

THE BLESSINGS OF FORGIVENESS:

Negative emotions strain us, and take away our spiritual desire for growth. If we ask for anything in God's name as sincere commandment keepers, He will do it for us, if it's in tune with His will. **Have faith! Stay faithful!** Give God your worries and burdens, those known and unknown. Purify your heart of all sins so you will receive the strength to sincerely forgive from the heart. Be joyous again, and be set free.

PRAYER OF HEALING!

Lord, I know that whenever I suffer, you experience my pain. You sympathize with me, because you suffered here on earth just for me. Please don't allow the negative things of my past to control me anymore. Cleanse me and remove all my sufferings! Remove any denial, defensiveness, or delusion from my past. Enable me to walk with the freedoms of the past, and hope for the future.

JOURNAL THOUGHTS

DEPRESSION

For I know the thoughts that I think toward you, saith the Lord, thoughts of peace, and not of evil, to give you an expected end.

Jeremiah 29:11

YOUR CHECK-UP:

HOW ARE YOU FEELING TODAY?

- ☐ Happy
- ☐ Sad
- ☐ Anxious
- ☐ Frustrated
- ☐ Stressed
- ☐ Angry
- ☐ Numb
- ☐ Content
- ☐ Peaceful

WHY?: _____
_____
_____

SYMPTOMS:
sadness, remorse, moody, anger, malice, regret, isolation, emptiness, low self-care, disease

Is Your Health Optimal?

"Cheerfulness is the principle ingredient in the composition of health"

Life sometimes can be unpredictable, but many of us expect the perfect, enjoyable, fairytale, only fun times, and never anticipating the opposite side of that spectrum. What can that look like? Worry, fear, distrust, bitterness, anger, resentment, negative thoughts, depression, or not having a desire to live!

Did you know many diseases suffered stem from depression? When we are constantly in a negative state of mind (gloomy, sad, etc.), this affects our spiritual health, and is often the underlying cause for many physical illnesses.

MAJOR DEPRESSION ...

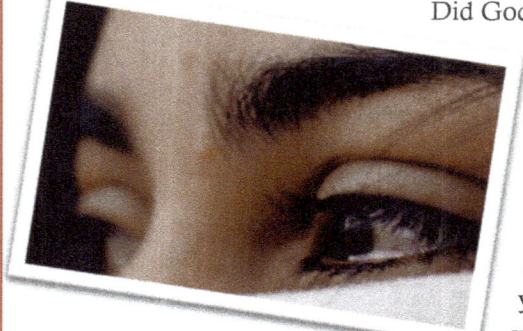

Did God create you to live in a state of unhappiness, darkness, numbness, or doom? There are times I have felt this way, having dark spirits around me. As a result, I struggled with getting out of bed, eating, bathing, etc. And in addition I remained isolated. These dark spirits would always encouraged me to give up on life, saying things such as, "You've tried long enough, you've failed at everything, why bother anymore?" "You're not worthy, you're not good enough, and the world will just go on without you." And after listening for a while, I agreed. I was a failure, no one loved me, and God surely didn't. How could He? Why would I feel like this every single day? **But, these are the lies of the enemy, to take your life.** Many times he wants us to be more critical of ourselves. Isaiah 41:10, comforts us to not be afraid or discouraged, because He is our God. **He will strengthen and help us!**

This was so true. Shortly after, God gave me a glimpse of hope. My peace came many times through crying (which is very therapeutic), writing, listening to uplifting songs, singing, taking a walk in nature, being still, or even just saying a quiet prayer: "Lord, help me to see Your love and hear Your voice of comfort." We must recognize that these are the times we need to especially hold on tightly to God's promises.

Imagine how Christ hurts when we hurt and weeps when we weep. He is constantly merciful and sympathetic toward our pain and broken heart. Isn't this an encouraging thought? Even better, it shows a deeper reflection of His loving character towards us!

When My Flashlight Grows Dim *(Poem)*

When a flashlight grows dim or quits working, do you just throw it away?
Of course not! You change the battery.
When a person messes up or finds themselves in a dark place, do you cast them aside?
Of course not! You help them change their batteries.

BATTERY TYPES:

Some need AA - Attention and Affection
Some need AAA - Attention, Affection, and Acceptance
Some need C - Compassion
Some need D - Direction

And if they still don't seem to shine, simply sit with them quietly and share your light.
– Rachel Dansby Freeman

FUNCTIONAL DEPRESSION ...

Functional depression can be a bit more alarming, and it harder to detect or even observe these symptoms. This condition allows those to suffer in silence while, on the surface, appearing happy or functional. They can be the life of the party, keeping business or home together, but when alone, they are dying inside. What a pretentious and exhausting life to live, having two identities. Are you overwhelmed, snappy, moody, numb, angry, or emotionally unavailable? A word of encouragement, stop suffering alone, stop pretending; this only hurts you in the end. Your life is being limited by your suffering, you keep up a wall from past hurts to avoid being hurt again, but you are simply living a life of imprisonment. How lonely and miserable this must be? Instead, keep your eyes on Christ. **He is everything!** When we focus on ourselves, we continue to worry about our circumstances, which produces feebleness of mind and disease.

Reflect upon the commandment we are breaking when we reside in depression. Could it be number eight, not stealing? Depression steals your joy, potential, purpose, opportunities, connections, hope, and your impact on the world. Don't allow this, instead; follow in the Savior's footsteps. His love is unfailing, especially during our emotional challenges and tears. Have compassion for yourself the same way He has already shown you. We should be inspired to trust God; He is your BEST support, so stay encouraged. Only then can we foster His peace.

Diet and Depression Correlation

There has been much research to show a correlation between poor nutrition and depression. So what is poor nutrition?

Foods that are processed, i.e. hot dog, pizza, fries, etc., low fiber, i.e. donuts, white bread, meat, etc., high sugar content, i.e. soda, ice-cream, energy drink, etc., high fat cholesterol, i.e., fast food, bacon, cheese, etc.

However, having a lifestyle with high fiber, plenty of water, exercise, sunshine, fresh air, etc., are just a few remedies to combat depression. **Take action!**

Frequent exercise is essential for managing low moods; it allows for your adrenaline and endorphins, which are the happy chemicals, to flow into your bloodstream. By raising your heart rate, it allows you to experience a more elevated demeanor. Try other uplifting activities such as: start a journal, sing a song, go into nature, memorize scripture, personally help someone in need, especially in the areas you are healing from. **This is a positive step toward recovery.** Remember also having a positive perspective that you will recover from depression and despair makes your recovery much more likely.

"Thank you, Lord, for Your continual love and hope!"

PEACE

Empathy Is Essential

Do you empathize with yourself? Many times we are too harsh on ourselves, this allows us to do the same with others. We need to end the cycle of negativity and not cultivate a diseased mind. Be determined to get out of the darkness so you can be restored for your impactful purpose.

Fervently repent and claim your loving heavenly Father's promises.

God is always there to comfort and listen to your deepest, aching prayers. At times, He may allow us to go through trials and anguish to develop our character and to get our attention. But, this draws us closer to Him and teaches us to depend on His power and strength.

Begin today to show yourself compassion and tenderness. Display your faith and belief in God; He is gracious and merciful unto you, willing to give you His peace. **So love yourself.**

PEACE that passes all understanding …

There is always hope in God, and no greater peace than having an intimacy with Christ. When you focus on your depression, you are only paying attention to your pains and struggles, and your eyes have left Christ's mercies. **You cannot heal this way!**

As God's children, deep down inside, we know we are not fully reliant on Him. But He sits patiently, waiting and longing for when you desire that intimate relationship with Him. He loves you so dearly and wants greatness for your life. You must **detox** your thoughts to experience the triumph that awaits you.

God's faithful prophet, **Elijah** struggled with depression. He was in despair, because he took his eyes off the faithfulness and power of God. Even after being used personally and seeing the great miracles of the mighty God, he believed the threatening words of man instead. This brought Elijah to the pit of destruction, even desiring death. Instead of believing God would protect him, he allowed fear to bring him into hopelessness, but our patient and merciful Savior sent an angel to comfort and minister to him. He was encouraged and strengthened, enabling Elijah to re-focus and cling to God for healing and victory.

God is waiting to do the same for you. To help you overcome challenges and receive the blessings of peace by holding onto His strength, as Isaiah 27:5 tells us. Let's continue to reflect on eternity with our merciful Savior. Or do you prefer to stay attached to this lost and fallen world?

"WHICH DO YOU CHOOSE?"

Christ, Our Example …

FROM GOD: **YOU ARE SPECIAL TO ME. YOU DESERVE PEACE!**

Pray unceasingly! We must agonize with Christ in wholehearted prayer. God will not turn us away and leave us void. He will instead give us the strength and power to overcome dark spirits, and release us from our greatest enemy. Imagine the prayers of Christ in the wilderness as He fasted for forty days. He submitted His will to God, which drew Him closer to His Father. Through this, He received the strength to overcome the enemy's temptations, even at His weakest point. Pray unceasingly for your healing and in your moments of doubt. Asking as Christ did, *"My God, my God, why hast thou forsaken me?"* (Matt. 27:46). **He will bring you peace and carry you through!** Then sing a song in your heart; you will feel the shadows of gloom begin to lift.

PEACE

YOU MUST DECIDE!

Many are allowing unforgiveness to turn into depression, which is simply anger turned inside out. The anger quietly fostered turns into sadness, gloom, and emotional destruction.

AFTER TIME WITH CHRIST:

HOW DO YOU FEEL?

- ☐ Happy
- ☐ Sad
- ☐ Anxious
- ☐ Frustrated
- ☐ Stressed
- ☐ Angry
- ☐ Numb
- ☐ Content
- ☐ Peaceful

COMMENT: _____
_____
_____

Your Prayer

_____
_____
_____

the OVERCOMER

Revelation 12:11

They overcame him by the blood of the lamb, and by the word of their testimony.

JUDGMENT

God's Spirit makes us loving, happy, peaceful, patient, kind, good, faithful, gentle, and self-controlled. There is no law against behaving in any of these ways.

Your Testimony

So many of us struggle, become sad, angry, broken, and at times numb to life. Why does God allow these difficulties to happen to us? We have been faithful to Him, haven't we? Isn't life supposed to be easier with Him?

The real question is: are these struggles to help us grow or others? The painful realization is they are certain to help both. Without our trials and circumstances, we would not grow in character. This is why during the difficulties, we become more dependent upon our Savior, haven't you noticed? Overcoming gives us an abundance of experiences to share with others of how to grow and overcome. Revelation 12:11 tells us we are to share our testimony to empower others and to help them mature for the kingdom. We are tested and tried daily, and only the faithful will overcome.

Your Salvation is worth the fight!

GOD WINS THE BATTLE!

Today's Date:_____   Goal Date:_____

SURRENDER

Commit to God all your faults, all your secrets, and all your unforgiveness…

FULLY OVERCAME

You did it! You stayed committed. Praise God for this victory! He has blessed you richly.

JOURNAL THOUGHTS

ANGER

SYMPTOMS:
hostile, inconsiderate, rude, impulsive, impatient, shameful, feeling unfairly treated, hateful, hurt, low self-respect

No man can serve two masters. For either he will hate the one, and love the other; or else he will hold to the one, and despise the other. You cannot serve God and money.
Matthew 6:24 MEV

YOUR CHECK-UP:

HOW ARE YOU FEELING TODAY?

- ☐ Happy
- ☐ Sad
- ☐ Anxious
- ☐ Frustrated
- ☐ Stressed
- ☐ Angry
- ☐ Numb
- ☐ Content
- ☐ Peaceful

WHY?: _____
_____
_____

Have you ever been impatient?

I'm sure you haven't, right? I must admit it wasn't my strong suit, and the Lord knows I have been guilty many times over. One of my favorite Bible characters is **Simon Peter**. He was so zealous for Christ, but he had a very harsh temper. John 18:10–11 reminds us how he did not hesitate to cut off the servant's ear when they came to arrest Christ. However, by the time Christ had finished ministering and teaching Peter, he was one of His most faithful and passionate disciple.

Who's Your Master?

Are you willing to fulfill your heavenly Father's will?

We must follow in our Savior's footsteps in all His ways. With the help of the Holy Spirit, this is the only way we will surrender our will,

to attain the fruits of the Holy Spirit, which includes patience.

We cannot be servants of Christ when we partake in gossip, impatience, hate, lust, selfishness, anger, envy, bitterness, and especially unforgiveness. Our verse for today reminds us in Matthew 6:24 that we cannot serve two masters. How can you serve Christ and sin? **This is not possible!** As servants of Christ, we will experience a constant nudging from the Holy Spirit to detest and abhor sin.

ANGER

The Demon Inside …

There are so many challenges we face in such a sinful world, a significant one being negative thoughts. I have allowed stress, anxiety, and high blood pressure to fester, because I thought the worst of someone's behavior toward me. But, God had to show me the real issue several times; it was myself. Often being offended, prideful, and unable to die-to-self, as Christ has asked us to.

Do you know the ugly demon within? Are you displaying an angel on the outside and a monster on the inside? Who does your family say you are: an undercover beast or a true Christian? From time to time, God allows us to see that we are **not** as reliant on Him as we think. If we relied on Him as we should, our thoughts would be more pure, our bodies healthier, and our minds at peace. We may not realize it, but many times when we get angry, it's because we are rejected, ashamed, hurt, or have unmet needs. In turn, we lash out at those around us or the situation. This is a sign of a deeper underlining wound. When **negative thoughts** attack you, ask yourself— are these thoughts of God? Then begin claiming a promise from God's word, *"Thou will keep him in perfect peace, whose mind is stayed on Thee."* (Isa.

Words of Wisdom Challenge!

 "We know that anger is usually derived from somebody wronging another person in some way, shape, or form. When the offender doesn't apologize, the victim usually holds a grudge. The longer it stays there, this grudge grows its roots within the person's mind. And if it hasn't happened already, it will transform into visible anger. Forgiveness doesn't aim to condone someone's behavior, forgive and forget what happened, restore trust, or do that person a favor. On the contrary, forgiveness aims to help us get rid of anger, attain better physical and mental health, and improve our lives. **Today, I challenge you to implement forgiveness into your life.** The benefits you see will surprise you more than you know." *~Ricky Brome II*

Satan definitely wants to change your love for God. Instead, he tempts and teaches you to distrust God's love and wisdom. Have you realized you're in a battle? He wants most of all for you to suffer with him on the Day of Judgment; he knows the magnificence and wonders of heaven and doesn't want you to enjoy that. So he deceives you into thinking the path he is offering is so much more pleasing and fulfilling. It's important to stay armed; reading and memorizing God's word, so when the difficult times come along, you have your spiritual ammunition ready. If you are taken down during battle, it's because you have not been strengthened spiritually, to be fully equipped for the enemy. Here are a few verses to meditate on in your moments of trials and temptations…

SCRIPTURES DURING LIFE'S DIFFICULT MOMENTS ...

- ✓ **ANGRY**: Proverbs 14:29 Whoever is patient has great understanding, but one who is quick-tempered displays folly. (NIV)

- ✓ **IMPATIENT**: Colossians 3:12 God chose you to be the holy people He loves, you must clothe yourselves with tenderhearted mercy, kindness, humility, … and patience. (NLT)

- ✓ **YOUR ENEMIES**: Psalm 25:2 I trust in you, My God! Do not let me be disgraced, or let my enemies rejoice in my defeat. Psalm 41:11 I know you are pleased with me, for you have not let my enemies triumph over me. (NLT)

- ✓ **PARENTING**: Psalm 119:169 Let my cry come before You, O Lord; Give me understanding according to Your word. (NKJV)

- ✓ **DOUBT**: Matthew 14:31 Jesus immediately reached out and grabbed him. "You have so little faith, … why did you doubt Me?" (NLT)

- ✓ **HATEFUL**: Psalm 119:133 Direct my steps by Your word, and let no iniquity have dominion over me. (NKJV)

- ✓ **MARRIAGE CHALLENGES**: Psalm 120:1 In my distress I cried to the Lord, and He heard me. (NKJV)

- ✓ **TEMPTATIONS**: John 16:33 In the world you will have tribulation; but be of good cheer, I have overcome the world. (NKJV)

- ✓ **PRIDEFUL**: Proverbs 16:5 The Lord detests the proud; they will surely be punished. (NLT)

- ✓ **TRIALS**: Psalm 57:1 Be merciful to me, O God, be merciful to me! For my soul trusts in you; and in the shadow of your wings I will make my refuge, until these calamities have passed by. John 16:33 I have spoken to you, that in me you may have peace. (NKJV)

- ✓ **NEGATIVE THOUGHTS**: Proverbs 4:23 Be careful how you think. Your thoughts make you the person that you are. (EASY)

- ✓ **ANXIOUS**: Psalm 94:19 When doubts filled my mind, your comfort gave me renewed hope and cheer. Psalm 55:22 Give your burdens to the Lord, and he will take care of you. He will not permit the godly to slip and fall. (NLT)

- ✓ **LOW SELF-WORTH**: 1 Peter 3:4 You should clothe yourselves instead with the beauty that come from within, the unfading beauty of a gentle and quiet spirit, which is so precious to God. (NLT)

- ✓ **REVENGE**: Romans 12:19 Never take revenge. Leave that to the righteous anger of God. For the Scriptures say, "I will take revenge; I will pay them back," says the Lord. (NLT)

- ✓ **HOPELESS**: Psalm 102:1 A prayer of one overwhelmed with trouble, pouring out problems before the Lord. Lord, hear my prayer! Listen to my plea! (NLT)

- ✓ **SELF-DOUBT**: Psalm 46:5 God is in the midst of her; she shall not be moved: God shall help her… (KJV)

- ✓ **ALONE**: Deuteronomy 31:6 Be strong and of good courage, do not fear nor be afraid of them; for the Lord your God, He is the One who goes with you. He will not leave you nor forsake you. (NKJV)

- ✓ **HEARTBROKEN**: Psalm 147:3 He heals the brokenhearted and bandages their wounds. (NLT)

- ✓ **SUICIDAL**: Psalm 25:17 The troubles of my heart have enlarged; bring me out of my distresses! Psalm 119:143 Trouble and anguish have overtaken me. Psalm 119:77 Let your tender mercies come to me, that I may live. Psalm 119:94 I *am* yours, save me. (NKJV)

PATIENCE

Release Your Anger!

We continue to live in violation of the one true love note God has left us, **His ten commandments.** We are choosing to live in disobedience. Oh, how we must displease our Savior through our thoughts, behavior, and heart.

Anger stems from many reasons and people: lack of love and attention, neglect, feeling unfairly treated, abused, being teased, controlled, manipulated, used, and so on. But the one that I've noticed most lasting, began in childhood by your parents or guardian. Whether you feel your anger is justified or not, this is heartbreaking to God. He never wants us to harbor anger, dragging it around for months and decades.

There are situations as children we've all gone through that were unfair to us, but we do not have to live there in anger. We must let go of the hurt because it continues to bring us pain frequently, as it steals our joy. It also outlines the way we interact with and treat others. We are frequently impatient, harboring anger, blaming others, staying a victim, or unable to forgive.

Who Are You Honoring?

When you violate the fifth commandment, which is honoring your parents that your days may be long upon the earth, this is also the only law with a promise. We know that as God's child, He always gives us the best. So when He says that your days may be long upon the earth, do you think he means in anger, bitterness, and emptiness? **Of course not!** How could we honor our

And, if you do not desire to honor your parents, you are living in anger by choice. *Remember Cain and Abel.* God does not desire for His precious children to live this way.

He has a life of abundance, joy, purpose, and optimal health prepared for us. He wants our mind and body to be a glorifying example to the world.

So even in a situation where distance is needed in a parent-child relationship, how can you honor them without disturbing your peace of mind? You can choose not to speak negatively about them, pray for them, and show respect. These actions, along with forgiveness, will prayerfully draw you closer to your parents (if they are still here).

Ephesians 4:31–32

> *Let all bitterness, and wrath, and anger, and clamour, and evil speaking, be put away from you, with all malice:*
> *And be ye kind one to another, tenderhearted, forgiving one another, even as God for Christ's sake hath forgiven you.*

PATIENCE

FROM GOD: ***DOES YOUR HEART LONG FOR MY PURPOSE?***

Christ, Our Example …

We must remember at all times that Christ is our ultimate example. Without gaining His humility and love, we will not be able to enter into His kingdom. Observe even His response to Peter's impulsive reaction (cutting off the ear), Christ **patiently** asked Peter, **"Should I not do the will of my Father?"** So even upon death, Christ was lovingly committed to fulfilling His Father's will.

It doesn't make a difference what you are going through right now, God will always love you and is willing to forgive you. He is only seeking for a sorrowful and repentant heart. When anger is stirred up inside you, resulting in an explosive temper, this sinful reaction prevents others and yourself from coming to Christ. You are unable to be the **light**, you are called to be. Here's my question, do you truly want to be free from the sinful thoughts that prevent you from walking closer with Christ?

Ask Him to *live out His life within you daily* so that you may receive the **reward** of heaven. He is waiting to heal your pain, heal your heart, and heal your mind.

Your Prayer

_____

_____, AMEN!

AFTER TIME WITH CHRIST:

HOW DO YOU FEEL?

- ☐ Happy
- ☐ Sad
- ☐ Anxious
- ☐ Frustrated
- ☐ Stressed
- ☐ Angry
- ☐ Numb
- ☐ Content
- ☐ Peaceful

COMMENT: _____

WHAT IS REPENTANCE?

Repentance requires conversion. Unbelief must be removed. Self must die!

Many are unaware that the Holy Spirit convicts us of sin, and this is what brings the desire to repent and obey God's pathway. As we repent, we must hunger for righteousness. The Holy Spirit then takes away our carnal desires for earthly things and fills us with the longing for holiness.

Many of us take advantage of the act of repentance, asking for forgiveness and never changing. But this is incorrect and deceiving to one's self. When we continue to be defiant and repeat the same sins, Christ holds us accountable since we have been given light on those sins. This behavior no longer allows the Holy Spirit to be able to convict or influence our spirit.

Do not conceal wrongs; confess them heartily and honestly, forsaking the desires for sin. When we repent, we leave sin (death) and enter into obedience (life). Our world becomes brighter and more at peace. Our mind becomes clearer by removing all the guilt we once willingly fostered. Now the Holy Spirit has taken hold of our lives and made it anew; from darkness to light, a change of negative thoughts to healthy thoughts, inward change, not just outwardly. This is when God can immensely use us to help those who are broken, and to give them Christ, as their hope and shield.

Focus on genuine repentance. Don't get caught up in the moment or excitement of emotional repentance; tears, shouts, elations, or public displays. We can fall easily into self-deception, so being honest with God will hurt at times, but trust Him. Psalm 139:23–24 (NRSV) reminds us to, *"Search me, O God, and know my heart; test me and know my thoughts. See if there is any wicked way in me, and lead me in the way everlasting."* Repentance shows a change in behavior, a difference others can see and hear.

A TRUE GODLY COUNTENANCE!

GODLY REPENTANCE	WORLDLY REPENTANCE
Willingly confesses sin and acknowledges guilt	Is defensive and argumentative; won't acknowledge guilt
Is angry about his own sin	Is angry at the one who exposes his sin
Fears the wrath and discipline of God	Fears exposure, shame, and loss of reputation
Longs to restore relationships broken by sin	Is apathetic about lost relationships
Is dedicated to and zealous for holiness	Has no interest in holiness; is attracted to the world
Is willing to make restitution for his sin	Is uncaring about the consequences of his sin and unwilling to make restitution
Is pure in all subsequent actions	His subsequent life is impure and ungodly

JOURNAL THOUGHTS

SELF-HATE

I love the Lord because he hears my voice and my prayer for mercy. Because he bends down to listen, I will pray as long as I have breath!
Psalm 116:1–2

YOUR CHECK-UP:

HOW ARE YOU FEELING TODAY?

- ☐ Happy
- ☐ Sad
- ☐ Anxious
- ☐ Frustrated
- ☐ Stressed
- ☐ Angry
- ☐ Numb
- ☐ Content
- ☐ Peaceful

SYMPTOMS:

anger, impatience, remorse, intolerance, low self-worth, selfishness, lack of sympathy, vengefulness, guilt, morbid thoughts

Have you noticed the way you treat others lately? Many times we treat others the way we treat ourselves. Whether it is unforgiveness toward others or we have not forgiven ourselves for our wrongs, unforgiveness is a disease that will cause physical and mental illnesses. Have you ever heard the famous saying, *"Treat others the way you want to be treated?"* It's actually a golden rule found in Luke 6:31. But, what many have not thought about regarding this phrase is; what if I don't love myself? You won't be able to show genuine love to someone else, and certainly not to your loving Savior. So, why are you unable to love yourself? Do you feel what you have done in the past is unworthy of God's forgiveness?

How can you cure this dark plague of paralysis?

Well, I have news for you, you're wrong. There is no sin that is too great for your Savior to forgive. Never feel as if you are unworthy of His love and mercy. So, how can you change if you don't believe that Christ has always loved you and has forgiven all your errors? When we dislike or hate ourselves, we do not see the blessings that God has in store for us. There is someone who had the same issue. Let's read in Matthew 27:3–5.

This is the story of **Judas Iscariot**, one of Christ's disciples who betrayed Him. But even Judas' sin was pardonable. If only he had truly repented and not focused on the guilt and shame, or other people's opinion of his betrayal. This should have been a dialogue between him and God alone. There is no sin too great that you cannot ask God to pardon. **None!**

SELF-HATE

I Love Me Today!

I love me today… because, God loves me the most. How can I be pleasing to Him and more confident in His love? Do you appreciate His love?

Show Him your grateful heart by blessing someone today.

I'm God's Favorite!

Digging Deeper

Self-hate stems from deep within. Many times we attribute it to how bitter people treat us (i.e., bullying at school, work, or, sadly, at church). Unfortunately, it goes back even further into our earlier years. How your guardians and family might have treated you growing up could negatively impact the view of who you are. This can create rage from built-up anger, violence, negative thoughts, and often self-hatred. You might feel unworthy of having good things or people in your life. Maybe you feel like a failure, feel unloved, are a loner and unable to connect deeply with others, or find it hard to accept compliments. This can all stem from being neglected, abused, and frequently spoken down to by the people that were meant to protect and love you the most. This is devastating to a child's self-esteem. Impacting their ability to be compassionate, respectful of others, friendships, business, and even in marriage. But sadly, our parents could not give what they didn't have. It's a fact that hurting people hurt people. How did their parents show them love and discipline? This is so much deeper than you or me; it's unfortunately a generational misfortune.

My Empty Tank …

I remember going through a relationship and looking for the love I lacked growing up, from my partner. I was hoping and expecting him to love and value me the way my parents didn't, but this was a disaster waiting to happen. It added so much pressure to the relationship that it eventually ended up in complete failure, leaving me feeling even more unworthy and unlovable. My anger and emptiness grew even more internally, further impacting my lack of self-worth. My needs were not met and my love tank was still not filled.

So I started to believe the negative thoughts in my mind. To stop them, I looked again for another relationship to validate me so I could finally be happy and fulfilled, as others appeared to be.

I had no clue then, but this was an unfair expectation. It was never my partner's duty. These emotions were unhealthy, unrealistic, and unbalanced. **Your worth can come only from the Savior!**
Not others, nor the world.

It Starts With A Decision

My behavior did not depict the real me: a treasure of Christ. I am more than worthy! Christ sacrificed His life to save my heart from this unloving and sinful world. ***All I need is His love!***

There is no love in this world that can replace His love. It will only be a temporary fix, and eventually, your heart will feel empty again. Think about this, you've probably already experienced this, so don't do it again to yourself. There is hope in your heavenly Father. You may not have had nurturing parents to love and validate you, but today, God is there to love and validate you. He is the only answer that can fill, **all your voids.**

Have you been feeling lost lately, empty, sad, angry, or maybe even ready to give up on life? I understand your pain; I've been there. Hold fast to God. In this uncertain time, remember, **He understands you Best!**

There is a greater purpose behind your pain. God has created you for greater things, to transform lives, to share hope, and to bring joy to the lost. You have been called to help those suffering emotionally **for such a time as this!** Through helping others, you begin to experience optimal health and a brighter, cheerful spirit.

Psalm 40 assures us that He will take us out of the pit of destruction, set our feet upon a rock and give us His purpose! We know that anything contradicting God's word or law is definitely from the enemy, and we need to run the other direction. Christ has died on the cross and broken all your generational curses, decide today to be the difference.
Be the bloodline breaker for your family.

Begin being compassionate and kind to yourself as Christ has. Avoid using your parents' wrongdoings as a crutch; this only hinders you from your life's potential. Your past does not need to dictate your future. Let go of it; it's stopping you from being the blessing you should be for others, and it's also stealing your joy.

Signs of Your Pain

Are you or a loved one addicted to shopping? Many times we tend to buy things trying to make ourselves feel better, but this is only a temporary solution. Sometimes this may not look like shopping but includes other addictions, such as food, impulsiveness, media, love of money, power, sex, status, and the list goes on.

When it comes to addictions, we are looking for comfort, relief, or connection, but instead, it brings only temporary fulfillment.

Here's what you need to do: ask God to help you submit, fervently repent, change your behavior, and commit to being an obedient follower of Christ.

This is all He wants from you, your loyalty and love. Find your worth in Christ! Give your heart and emotional pain to the **only** source of healing, **Your Savior!**

Trust Him!
He never leads you astray.

ONLY GOD CAN FILL AN EMPTY HEART
Psalm 4

KIND NESS

Thoughts of Peace

As you go throughout your day, reflect upon one devotional thought and scripture. Think about the peace that Christ had, even as He was ridiculed and sacrificially died for **YOU!** *He found you to be* **worthy** *of saving and worthy of being in His kingdom. You must now do your part and remain faithful unto Him.*

This Could Be Life Or Death!

Let us not displease our Savior with negative self-talk or thoughts; we would be neglecting the second commandment in this situation—thou shalt not make any graven image. By making ourselves idols, we focus too much on our insufficiencies or have constant negative thoughts about ourselves (even if someone else planted those terrible thoughts from earlier on). There will always be people around to speak negatively, creating self-doubt in many and even thoughts of hating one's self and not feeling worthy enough. This is why **healing is so imperative.**

Do not allow this false limiting belief to overtake your mind. This is the enemy's trap and mission. There may be times when self-hate can spiral into a darker space, where morbid thoughts about taking your life are the result. Someone might desire to escape their pain and emotions, but this is a permanent decision to a temporary problem.

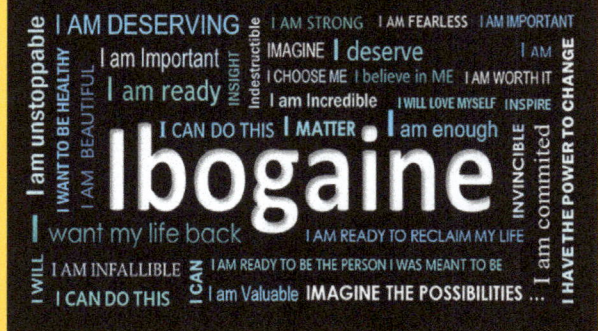

You may not feel important enough to yourself as to why you desire to make such a decision, but you are more than deserving to be here for Christ. If you are overwhelmed, cry out to God first. He is waiting on your call, waiting to rescue you. Your life is so valued you have been designed for greatness and to impact the world with God's love.

*IMPORTANT: If you are in need of someone to talk to, please call the crisis hotline at **800.273.8255** anytime to speak with an advisor. Support is there for you, waiting to help you. Also, check the resource section of this book for more encouraging words and songs. Find a community that will support and encourage you to begin living life again. Your community is essential to your healing, remove yourself from negativity and align yourself with positive people. **This is essential.** God needs you, and until you completely surrender, there is no peace!

KINDNESS

CHRIST, OUR EXAMPLE ...

Christ gives us the recipe for attaining kindness and **J.O.Y**:
(J)esus first,
(O)thers second, and then
(Y)ourself.

When we put Him first, He multiplies all the love we have given Him and returns it for us to share bountifully with others and ourselves. This helps us to esteem Christ and love Him more, even before ourselves.

As Christ was here during His ministry, He blessed and brought great joy to those He gave a helping hand to, as He healed and also forgave.

Anything that contradicts God's word is from the enemy. We know that Christ brings unity, and the enemy teaches division, unforgiveness, self-exaltation, pain, and selfish self-focus.

WHOSE PATH WILL YOU CONTINUE TO TAKE?

AFTER TIME WITH CHRIST:

HOW DO YOU FEEL?

- ☐ Happy
- ☐ Sad
- ☐ Anxious
- ☐ Frustrated
- ☐ Stressed
- ☐ Angry
- ☐ Numb
- ☐ Content
- ☐ Peaceful

COMMENT: _____
_____
_____

YOUR PRAYER

_____
_____
_____
_____
_____
_____
_____
_____, AMEN!

FROM GOD:
THE LOVE I HAVE FOR YOU IS CONSTANT AND EVERLASTING.

ARE YOU READY TO GIVE UP?

DON'T GIVE IN

LIFE OR DEATH?

Life can be challenging. It might feel hopeless right now with no end in sight. Still, **DON'T GIVE UP!**

When you are tempted to give up on life, ready to feel no more pain, maybe even hating yourself, **HOLD ON EVEN TIGHTER!** I've been there.

In the midst of your tears, stop your thoughts from focusing on self and lift your eyes up to Christ. Feel the sorrow and pity He has for your broken heart. Cry out to Him! He is waiting to rescue you.

Do you know the road of hope designed for you and the numerous lives He has for you to change? Remember the sacrifice of Christ. All for you!

Should your emotions control you or should your will-power? The power of will improves the health of your body and the mind. Emotions should not dictate if your day is pleasant or moody. This will produce a life of unpleasant roller-coaster rides.

Christ does not present to His followers the hope of attaining earthly glory and riches, nor of living a life free from trials.

Instead, He calls us to follow Him in the path of self-denial & humility. Ask God and be willing to follow His will and way. He will reveal it to you.

Let go of the things in your past. Forgive yourself for the poor decisions of the past and then release them. Get out of your imprisonment. Dragging around the burdens of your past will prevent you from living God's purpose-filled life.

1 Corinthians 13:5 reminds us, *"Love thinks no evil."* This includes no negative thoughts against self. Surrender your will.

When we are imprisoned, burdened, unforgiving, hurt, and resentful, we live a life of captivity instead of freedom. But, with the love and grace of Christ, you will overcome.

"Forgiveness is recognizing that God is stronger than the people that have wounded you."
-Dr. Neil Nedley

YOU MATTER

You matter to God — Isa. 49:16

JOURNAL THOUGHTS

SELFISHNESS

Now when Jesus heard these things, He said unto him, Yet lackest thou one thing: sell all that thou hast, and distribute unto the poor, and thou shalt have treasure in heaven: and come, follow me.
Luke 18:22

SYMPTOMS:

resentment,
hurt,
hateful,
unforgiveness,
indifference,
feeling unloved,
feeling unaccepted,
unconverted,
distrustful,
low self-confidence

YOUR CHECK-UP:

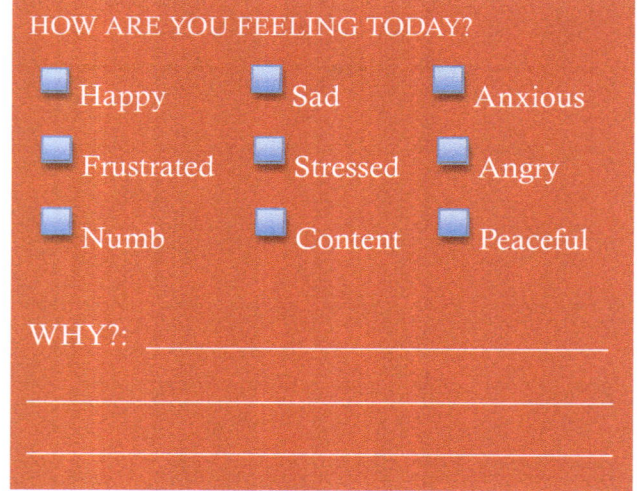

HOW ARE YOU FEELING TODAY?
- ☐ Happy
- ☐ Sad
- ☐ Anxious
- ☐ Frustrated
- ☐ Stressed
- ☐ Angry
- ☐ Numb
- ☐ Content
- ☐ Peaceful

WHY?: _____
_____
_____

Our World Today!

There are so many demands in our world today that we aren't aware of. It has become such a norm that we have just adapted to them as part of our lives. There is unlimited communication access to us: emails, texts, video calls, and of course, the age-old phone calls (if those still exist in this era). We have become so busy as a society that we have been robbed of our ability to care for others and have lost some of our interpersonal connections. We frequently hear the famous phrase, "I'm doing me!" However, this selfish mindset allows us to fall away from Christ. How can we avoid falling into the trap of only thinking of ourselves?

SELFISHNESS

Where is Your Treasure?

Do you believe a selfish man can enter into the gates of heaven? Luke 18:18–30 gives us an example of a **Certain Ruler**, who found it difficult to deny self and depend solely on God, even after contemplating his eternal reward. Read this story slowly and absorb why it was such a struggle for this man of status and wealth, to deny himself and the world. *"For where your treasure is, there will your heart be also."* Matthew 6:21

Was it that he wasn't doing enough for others or giving to the poor? No, this was much more profound than that. Just listen to Christ's response. He stated, **"Yet you lack one thing!"** What was that one thing the ruler lacked? He lacked complete surrender, a self-sacrificing attitude, true love for Christ, and an ability to show genuine love to his neighbors. He had an unconverted heart, so Christ was unable to influence him. He was doing it all for show, trying to gain heavenly treasures. **Could we be lacking that one thing today?**

We must give up our love for worldly attractions and unholy ambitions so that we may find our heavenly treasure. Selfishness steals our desire to help those around us who are suffering. We often justify why we should be placed first. Unwilling to help others, we lose out on sharing hope, wisdom, and the gift of eternal life. Do you desire to be an **almost** Christian or a converted one?

"Let us not do so much lip service, let us do more heart service." ~Pastor William Linthicum
Matthew 15:8

Have you noticed many times we transfer what we reflect without knowing? Do you have a cold demeanor that keeps people away from you? This is hindering your influence for good. Are encountering people with the same disposition, maybe an environment that is unsympathetic, unloving, or even hostile? This is because of the dark contagious spirit you might be wearing.

Your attitude displays the real person you are on the inside. If you have a selfish heart, you essentially need to ask God for healing from this spiritual hindrance. Acknowledge your ways of selfishness, and relinquish them. Do not continue to tearfully break the heart of your Savior any longer. *"Inasmuch as ye did it not to one of the least of these, ye did it not to me"* (Matt. 25:45).

RECIPE FOR SELF-LESS-NESS

Have you gotten the answer yet as to why we struggle with dying to self?

Submit yourself to the Lord. Selfishness is not of His spirit. We have fallen into such a Godless society, even within our church. You might say, that's not me; I believe in God. But, being of God means not only believing in Him. It also means also being like Him: kind, merciful, giving, and selfless. God is not our genie. Do not claim Him only when He benefits you. Instead, be bold for God and a faithful, committed witness.

Selfishness comes in many practices, but how about in the form of adultery? This is an inconsideration of God's seventh commandment. This is not only hurtful and selfish to those involved but wounding to God's heart. Needing to find validation because of your insecurities, from someone who is already involved, is dishonest, harmful, and not glorifying to your Heavenly Father. We cannot hide our selfish hearts from God, He already knows us inside and out. We need to admit our ways, so we can be renewed and set free.

Give Him Anything!

You will give GOD EVERYTHING, when you believe He is EVERYTHING!

We must choose to give up the world; it only deceives us into superficial fulfillments. It enslaves us into continually striving for the next aspiration, yet still feeling unfulfilled. *"Submit yourself therefore to the Lord..."* (James 4:7) We must die of self! **Give Up Your Control.** In the story of sincere Hannah she was not worried about what she needed anymore. Her prayer, faith, and praises in 1 Samuel 2 allowed her to completely surrender and receive a renewed peace from God. Just as Christ also emptied Himself to His Father even being obedient unto death, so you also should be willing to give up your life to Him (Mark 8:35). **Surrendering is required daily!** Christ is calling for you. Commit to a new prayer life; He is ready to restore you.

Cling tightly to your prayer life and renew your mind in Christ each day. When feelings lead us astray, we have placed them above the scripture and not died to self. The enemy plays on this. When we have died to self, those feelings are now used to glorify God. So make a sacrifice and confess the things that are separating you from God. He is waiting to bring you through, to give you a new life. **Eternal life!**

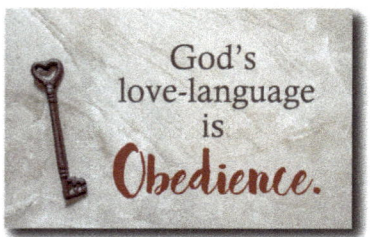

Don't let the enemy clog your ears from hearing God's voice. If we live inwardly, our lives become routine, boring, empty, anxious, and lifeless. But a life of Christ becomes expansive. When you have the identity of Christ, you live larger than yourself. Trust patiently in the Lord, and tell Him each morning, **"Lord, I am Yours."**

Then will your life become brighter, joyous, and purpose driven.

FROM GOD: DOES YOUR HEART LONG FOR MY PURPOSE?

HOW EASY IS IT TO SURRENDER?

Most find it difficult to give up control, including those with a challenging childhood or other types of trauma. But we must learn to give our heavenly Father full control of our lives. Our purpose is manifested through His will and our experiences.

Obedience must come from a heart of **Love**, and a willingness to surrender **All**.

Rewards of Un-selfishness

- ❖ Thoughtful
- ❖ Helpful
- ❖ Peaceful
- ❖ Generous
- ❖ Less stressed
- ❖ Kindhearted
- ❖ Honorable
- ❖ Forgiving
- ❖ Inclusive
- ❖ Empathic
- ❖ Welcoming
- ❖ Thankful
- ❖ No desire for gossip

I SURRENDER …

MY PRAYER FOR US

Dear heavenly Father, renew Your spirit within our hearts and minds. Restore us from all hurts and pains, and remove the shadows of the enemy from our lives. You understand what we lack and know how to provide for all our needs.

Begin our healing today, Lord, as we hold on to all Your promises. Help us to deny ourselves for the sake of others and not to neglect our brothers and sisters who are also drowning in problems. We know Your Word never lies, so we hold fast to Your truth for wisdom and strength. **Amen!**

Goodness
Galatians 5:22-25

Christ, Our Example ...

*Why do we struggle with dying to self? Why is it a challenge in today's world to do **good** for others? Why do we struggle to put a smile on someone's face? Why does selfishness seep into the heart so easily? Where does that spirit come from? Is this a spirit of Christ or the enemy?*

In Matthew 15:32, we find the story of Jesus speaking to the multitude for three days. Remember how hungry the crowd was, including Christ and His disciples? He could have said, "Send them away to eat, and we will go find our own food." But instead, He compassionately said, *"I will not send them away fasting, lest they faint."* Christ placed the multitude ahead of Himself, which included over 4,000 people. He had a self-less nature and was willing to serve others before His own needs. *This is a spirit of goodness, of selfless love!*

AFTER TIME WITH CHRIST:

HOW DO YOU FEEL?

☐ Happy ☐ Sad ☐ Anxious

☐ Frustrated ☐ Stressed ☐ Angry

☐ Numb ☐ Content ☐ Peaceful

COMMENT: _____
_____
_____

Your Prayer

_____
_____
_____
_____
_____
_____, AMEN!

WHAT ARE SINS OF THE FLESH?

Now the works of the flesh are manifest, which are these; Adultery, fornication, uncleanness, lasciviousness, Idolatry, witchcraft, hatred, variance, emulations, wrath, strife, seditions, heresies, Envyings, murders, drunkenness, revellings, and such like: of the which I tell you before, as I have also told you in time past, that they which do such things shall not inherit the kingdom of God.

Galatians 5:19–21

GALATIANS 5:19–21	ADDITIONAL
ADULTERY (Married)	PRIDE
FORNICATION (Unmarried)	GLUTTONY
UNCLEANNESS (Unholiness)	LYING
LASCIVIOUSNESS (Lustfulness)	UNFORGIVENESS
IDOLATRY	GREED
WITCHCRAFT	IMPATIENCE
HATEFUL	GOSSIP
VARIANCE (Discord)	COMPLAINING
EMULATION (Conflict)	VENGEANCE
WRATH (Sinful Anger)	MALICE
STRIFE	DECEIVING
SEDITIONS (Contentious)	LAZINESS/IDLENESS
HERESIES (Error in Religion)	NEGATIVE THOUGHTS
ENVY (Jealousy)	LUST
MURDER	ABUSE
DRUNKENESS	ADDICTIONS
REVELING (Riotous)	STEALING

SIN SEPARATES US!

When we disobey, we reject God and wander away from Him.
But, once we repent, we begin an intimacy with Him. Our biggest obstacle to discerning God's will is having our **own desires**. In pleasing our own hearts, we hurt His.
How can we continue to walk away from the Source of Life? **PRIDE IS OUR HINDERANCE!**

JOURNAL THOUGHTS

ANXIETY

Now faith is the substance of things hoped for,
the evidence of things not seen.

Hebrews 11:1

SYMPTOMS:

worry, doubt, anger, fear, moodiness, hate, digestive issues, depression, heart palpitations, impatience

YOUR CHECK-UP:

HOW ARE YOU FEELING TODAY?

- ☐ Happy
- ☐ Sad
- ☐ Anxious
- ☐ Frustrated
- ☐ Stressed
- ☐ Angry
- ☐ Numb
- ☐ Content
- ☐ Peaceful

WHY?: _____
_____
_____

The call came in very early one Friday afternoon, immediately triggering my anxiety. I was so stricken by fear that I couldn't check the message until Monday. This was a dispute that had been going on for over three months. My responses were delayed, and I had been crippled with worry.

IS ANXIETY CONTROLLING YOUR LIFE?

How much longer would this go on? The message was worse than I expected. It was regarding the police serving me with orders for court. Needless to say, my feelings of fear and worry magnified instantly. I wanted to sink into the ground or just disappear; anything but face the monster ahead of me!

I was getting tired of being controlled by the uncertainty of life. Satan had me in his palm for far too long. It's interesting, as Christians we claim to trust in God, but when the true test comes along, we allow the spirit of darkness (Satan) to take over our entire being, and God seems so far away. Sadly, we doubt His strength.

Our scripture today reminds us that we must hold on to God even when the evidence of victory **cannot** be seen!

So how do we overcome the condemnations of this world?

ANXIETY

There are many pressures and stresses that fall on us today. And the story of **Jacob** reminds us how we must earnestly wrestle the past sins and anxieties of our soul.

Jacob remembered the sins of his youth, which tormented him for decades. When it was time for him to meet his brother Esau again, fear and anxiety took control of his mind and body. He feared for his life.

In order to not be overcome by fear, he had to confess all his wrongful behaviors and the injustices he had done to his own brother. He begged and pleaded with God all night. Without this blessing and mercy, Jacob thought, surely, Esau would have killed him upon sight. But, because of his faith and determination for God's blessing, he wrestled all night. His sincere confession finally granted him mercy.

Why is surrendering so difficult for you? Who do you trust, yourself or God? Do you feel that there are things you can't give up? Maybe your own idols you've created: status, money, bitterness, social media, unforgiveness, a relationship, addictions, gossip, or sexual immoralities?

Surrendering means letting go of your abilities and being vulnerable with God. It is our fears, anxiety, and unbelief that prevents us from giving up what God has asked us to give Him. That "thing" means too much to us, plus giving it up means we will be relinquishing our joys and control. But, this is a lie!

We simply do not believe our God is big enough to replace what he's asked us to sacrifice for Him. Christ's love is unwavering … so receive His bountiful freedom instead.

ARE YOU WILLING TO WRESTLE WITH GOD? (Gen 32:24–30)

CHECKLIST:
- Hourly
- Daily
- Weekly
- Monthly
- Yearly

WHO ARE YOU BATTLING WITH?

Self is the most challenging persona to handle. Many times control is important to us. This is due many times to a childhood trauma, not having control or protection as a child. As Christians, we may come to Christ during our struggles and burdens to lay them at His feet, but will neglect to daily surrender self at the throne.

Satan takes advantage of our lack of faith and ignorance. Faith is not a feeling or emotion. Faith is a decision to trust God at His word. If your faith is shaky or fragile, more time is needed in the Word. Memorize a scripture that takes you through the week; it is your armor and shield of survival.

When we are constantly in a state of anxiety, we can look at this as taking the Lord's name in vain, God's third commandment. Expressing our faith in Him but relying on self, this becomes just a vain repetition when asking for His help due to our constant worry and disbelief. We have the luxury of staying in anxiety because there is no real danger, but worrying does not solve the problem at hand it only stresses and disconnects you from God's love and strength.

Put your confidence in God during uncertain times, surrender, and lean on His wisdom and direction for your life. We need to search deeply in our hearts, and empty our minds from worry and anxiety. Instead, find someone to support you and stop looking to your own abilities. **God will fill All Your Voids!**

Choose Healing!

Surrendering is admitting that you don't have control because you have never been in control. Remember, there is always power in tears.

God can now do more for you and give you His power to heal. Experience His pardoning grace and love. What an exciting reality.

I Didn't Quit ... I Surrendered!

FAITHFULNESS

"YOU ARE AFRAID TO SURRENDER BECAUSE YOU DON'T WANT TO LOSE CONTROL! **BUT YOU NEVER HAD CONTROL …** ALL YOU HAD WAS ANXIETY." -Elizabeth Gilbert

Answered Prayers

Date: _____

Date: _____

Date: _____

Date: _____

The Power of Tears

Why do we cry? We cry because we are sad or fed up. We cry because we are hurt and lonely. We cry because we have been betrayed or disillusioned. We cry because we have regret; we wonder why, how, where, what. We cry because … well, sometimes we don't even know why we are crying! If you have ever cared for a baby, you know the stress of trying to figure out why the child is crying, especially after you have fed them, changed them, and put them down for a nap! Sometimes they just want to be held. Similarly, sometimes we, too, want to be held in the embrace of God but are conscious of our sinfulness that seems to distance us from Him. Read more at https://shalomtidings.org/the-power-of-tears/

When we cry, it releases endorphins and oxytocin, which are our natural happy and calming hormones. These help to reduce your emotional pain and improve your mood, placing you in a more relaxed state of mind.

OUR FINAL HOME

THIS IS NOT OUR FINAL HOME. CHRIST IS ALREADY PREPARING A PLACE FOR US. ONCE WE FULLY SURRENDER AND REMAIN FAITHFUL, WE ARE SURE TO ENJOY LIFE ETERNAL WITH HIM!

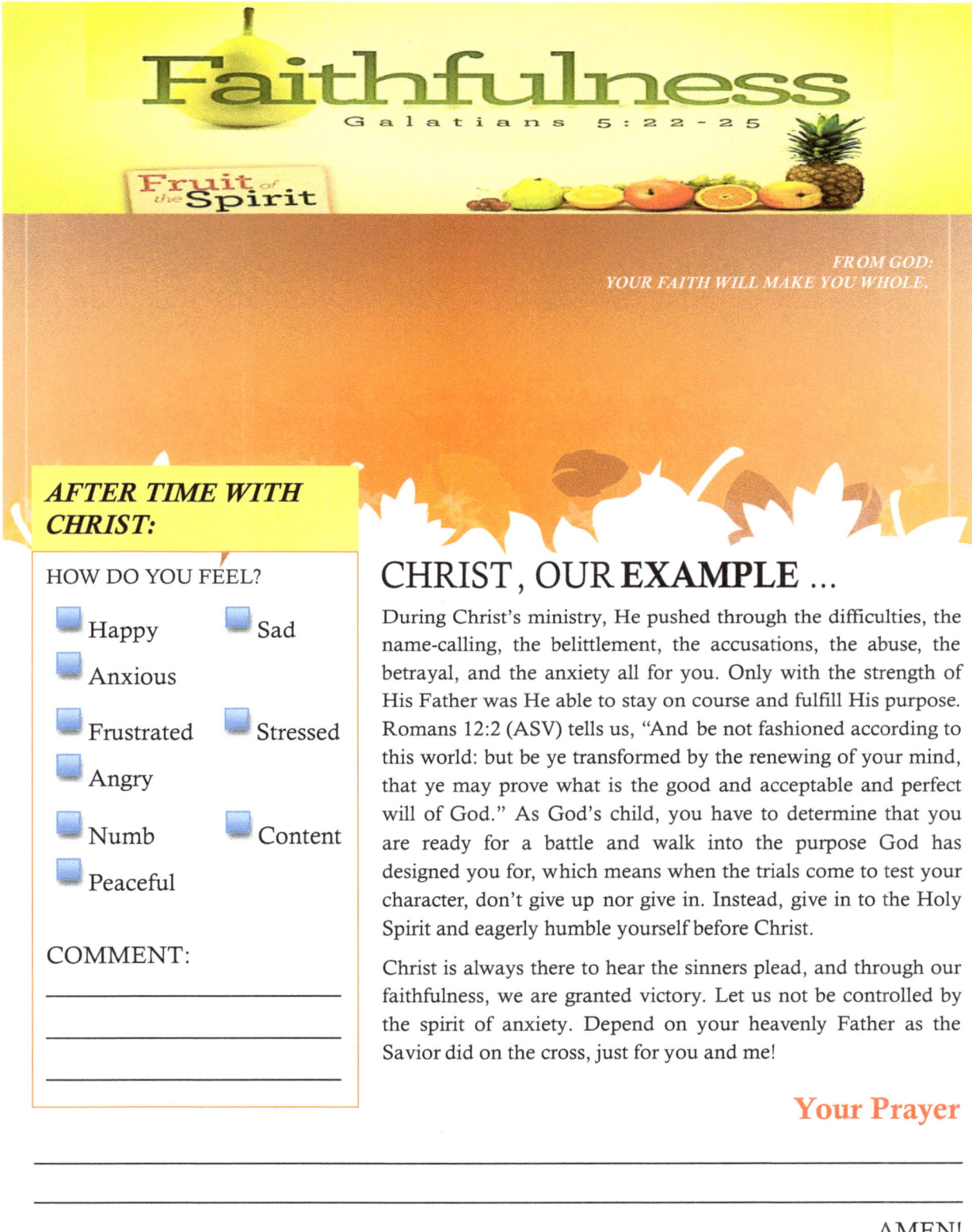

FROM GOD:
YOUR FAITH WILL MAKE YOU WHOLE.

AFTER TIME WITH CHRIST:

HOW DO YOU FEEL?

- ☐ Happy
- ☐ Sad
- ☐ Anxious
- ☐ Frustrated
- ☐ Stressed
- ☐ Angry
- ☐ Numb
- ☐ Content
- ☐ Peaceful

COMMENT:
_____
_____
_____

CHRIST, OUR **EXAMPLE** …

During Christ's ministry, He pushed through the difficulties, the name-calling, the belittlement, the accusations, the abuse, the betrayal, and the anxiety all for you. Only with the strength of His Father was He able to stay on course and fulfill His purpose. Romans 12:2 (ASV) tells us, "And be not fashioned according to this world: but be ye transformed by the renewing of your mind, that ye may prove what is the good and acceptable and perfect will of God." As God's child, you have to determine that you are ready for a battle and walk into the purpose God has designed you for, which means when the trials come to test your character, don't give up nor give in. Instead, give in to the Holy Spirit and eagerly humble yourself before Christ.

Christ is always there to hear the sinners plead, and through our faithfulness, we are granted victory. Let us not be controlled by the spirit of anxiety. Depend on your heavenly Father as the Savior did on the cross, just for you and me!

Your Prayer

_____
_____
_____, AMEN!

CONSEQUENCES OF UNFORGIVENESS

Guilt, regret, resentment, grievances, sadness, bitterness, and all forms of

NON –FORGIVENESS

are caused by too much past, and not enough present.

MENTALLY	PHYSICALLY	SPIRITUALLY
GUILT	INDIGESTION	NO DEVOTIONAL LIFE
RESENTMENT	MUSCLE PAIN	LACK OF FAITH
ANGER	HEART ATTACK	MINIMAL/NO PRAYER LIFE
PRIDEFULNESS	NIGHTMARES	INDIFFERENT
IMPATIENCE	CANCER	DISTRUST IN GOD
BITTERNESS (MALICE)	FREQUENT HEADACHES/ MIGRAINES	STUNTED SPIRITUAL GROWTH
STUBBORNESS	ULCER	STRIFE/DISCORD
MOOD SWINGS	DEPRESSION	WITHDRAWN
LOW SELF-WORTH	HIGH BLOOD PRESSURE	UNIMPACTFUL DEVOTION
PARANOIA	GASTRITIS	DOUBTFUL
NEGATIVE THINKING	LONELINESS	UNSYMPATHETIC
ADDICTIONS	STROKE	TAINTED VIEW OF GOD
VICTIM MINDSET	HEART DISEASE	UNLOVING
OVERREACTING	COLITIS	HARSHNESS
BLAMING/ACCUSING	ANXIETY	INTEMPERANCE
SUICIDAL THOUGHTS	OBESITY	NO INTEREST IN SPIRITUAL THINGS
NARCISSISM	HALLUCINATIONS	DEMON POSSESSION
SELFISHNESS	ACID REFLUX	LOVE OF GOSSIP
HATEFUL/VENGEFUL	POST TRAMATIC STRESS DISORDER (P.T.S.D.)	BELIEVE GOD DOESN'T EXIST

JOURNAL THOUGHTS

PRIDE

When pride cometh, then cometh shame: but with the lowly is wisdom.

Proverbs 11:2

SYMPTOMS:

anger, hurt, grief, hateful, disrespectful, harsh, selfish, stubborn, arrogant, unforgiveness

What is pride? Is it blatant or subtle? Have you experienced pride, or do you consider yourself more humble?

YOUR CHECK-UP:

HOW ARE YOU FEELING TODAY?

- ☐ Happy
- ☐ Sad
- ☐ Anxious
- ☐ Frustrated
- ☐ Stressed
- ☐ Angry
- ☐ Numb
- ☐ Content
- ☐ Peaceful

WHY?: _____
_____
_____

WHERE DOES YOUR PRIDE STEM FROM?

Proverbs 16:18 tells us pride comes before destruction, and a haughty spirit before a fall. **How Interesting!**

Let's look at one story in the Bible that we can learn from-- the great King Nebuchadnezzar in Daniel 4:37. He praises the mightiness of the King of heaven, and talks about God humbling you if you walk in pride. Later in Daniel 5:20–21, because of his haughtiness, God had to humble him greatly.

Pride can subtly creep into our hearts without us knowing. **Hurt can turn into pride.** Be watchful and give your hurts to the Lord.

He understands your pains, hurts, losses, & mental struggles. He eagerly waits for you to speak to Him. **Share your difficulties with Him today!**

I remember being used emotionally and financially by a close friend a few years ago. To protect myself, I ended the relationship, yet I kept in the hurt. I never allowed myself to grieve the loss of the friendship.

LIST TO SURRENDER

_____

_____

_____

How Big Is Your Wall?

I built up a wall and I told myself it would never happen again. This ignited and intensified the roots of pride. What I didn't know was how angry, prideful, and sensitive I became over time, even towards others. I didn't even trust God to help me. I was handling it myself. Now the new prideful me, was negatively impacting my faith and relationship with God.

"In keeping others out we are really imprisoning ourselves!"
~Anna Chiarenza

Even during your moments of pride, fears, disappointments, and grief, trust God! Many times we behave as an ungrateful and entitled generation, but our God is so longsuffering, as He wants to see all He has sacrificed for not to perish. Develop a spirit of gratitude to a God so merciful and patient with His children.

Jesus tells us in John 14:13–15 to ask God for anything in His name and it will be answered.

This is a prayer of assurance and comfort that when we learn to rely on God and humble self, He will fulfill His promises and take care of us.

Do not allow the way people badly treat you to impact your relationship with God. Then you'll be the one missing out on all His abundant blessings He's waiting to bestow upon you. Their behavior is not of His character, but of the wicked one. God only wants the best for you. Just believe Him!

SIGNS YOU ARE TOO SENSITIVE

- ❖ Easily offended and hurt
- ❖ Feeling like a failure
- ❖ Take things personal ly
- ❖ Prone to negative thinking
- ❖ Critical of self and others
- ❖ Holds a grudge, unforgiving
- ❖ Low sense of value/ self-worth
- ❖ Quick to put yourself down
- ❖ Over analyze r
- ❖ Self-conscious
- ❖ Maybe self -harm

WILL YOU OBEY HIM?

Many people are broken, they don't truly know God. Let go of the captivity they have placed on your life, they are simply allowing the enemy to use them. This is a spiritual battle. Let God win your battles. Give Him your heart and mind; this is the only way forgiveness is possible. Don't let your offender continue to rule your life, your happiness, your connections, or your purpose. Once God as ordained greatness over your life, no one can change that.

God brings us peace if we choose to accept it instead of focusing on the pains. Remember, there are three phases in life, we are either going into a storm, in the middle of a storm, or coming out of a storm. So, if we are experiencing difficulty or trials, remember if God takes us to it, He will bring us through it.

It's sometimes hard to accept that the bad things we have experienced in life have made us who we are today. But if it's still painful for you to accept, ask daily for a

GOD COMFORTS US AS A FRIEND...

submission of self. God will start to remove the hurts and pain. Then His ultimate sufferings will become more prominent in your heart, your pains will begin to heal and empathy for others will begin to grow again.

There was purpose in your pain, giving you the ability to and unhealed perspective, others cannot see the light of Christ in you or look to you for comfort. You choose whether your unfortunate situations will develop a positive character for the world, or continue to live in an imprisoned mind.

HUMBLE

FAITHFUL JOB

It's so sweet when your only hope is in Christ Jesus. Can you imagine life without Him? How much more desolate this world would be, and how unbearable your grief and troubles would be. Praise your dear, merciful Savior for all the tender and compassionate love He bestows upon you daily.

Job gives us this example in Job 23:10 –12 where he remained humble. He chose to trust God, rather than allow his grief to become pride, even though his closest friends and wife encouraged him not to. God knows your deepest desires and your darkest despairs. Come to Me, and I will give you strength. Give God the opportunity to brag on you, as He did with His faithful servant Job. Do not let pride and embarrassment hinder you from receiving God's blessings.

DO YOU KNOW GOD?

The negative things you allow to take hold of your mind are what distresses you the most. Stop justifying the way you are because of the hurts in your life, and don't be a **but** Christian (but I'm this way because of that, **but** it's not my fault, **but** it's her responsibility, etc.). You are only pleasing the enemy. This is hindering you from growing and flourishing; instead, be glorifying to God and grateful each day.

He knows what's best for your good; trust His ways. It takes effort to get to know God. He is your healer, provider, comforter, and friend. There is nothing you can do to gain God's love. He is the only one that gives you good things; all your talents and abilities are gifts from Him and to be used for Him.

Faith is not a happy feeling or emotion, but a decision to take God at His word. Do not let negative people influence you, as their faith is very little. By faith, you behold Him, and as He heals your plagues, your faith is strengthened and transformed. Walk closer with Him; you will have a better advantage in life.

God is waiting to enter your heart. Why don't you let Him come in? Are you ready to heal, to go from bondage to blessings? To trust God and not man, you must shift your belief system from crippled to conqueror, trauma to triumphant, and from victim to victorious!

We need to have far less confidence in what man can do and far more confidence in what God can do for every believing soul. He longs to have you to reach after Him by faith. He longs to have you except great things from Him.
Daughters of God 235.1

FROM GOD:
TRUST IN ME. I WILL REMOVE YOUR SORROW AND GIVE YOU COMFORT.

YOUR PRAYER

_____
_____

AFTER TIME WITH CHRIST:

HOW DO YOU FEEL?

- ☐ Happy
- ☐ Sad
- ☐ Anxious
- ☐ Frustrated
- ☐ Stressed
- ☐ Angry
- ☐ Numb
- ☐ Content
- ☐ Peaceful

COMMENT:
_____
_____
_____
_____

Christ, Our Example ...

Our Savior was surely the greatest example of humility, even during the anguish, depression, and anxiety that accumulated in the Garden of Gethsemane. Luke 22:42–44 tells us of the distress Christ went through even for you. Imagine the feeling of abandonment from those He wanted to save: His followers denied Him and the painful separation from His Father. Christ felt alone and unappreciated while sacrificing for such a prideful world.

In His despair, He clung to His Father, (see John 8:29). There is much hope knowing that Christ understands the prideful heart that keeps you hostage. Who better to lean on than the Rock that overcame the struggle you are still tormented with?

True character reveals itself in a crisis. What comes out of our mouths reflects our thoughts, and our thoughts affect our words, which influences our actions. Don't get caught up in someone's bad attitude; don't let other people control you. We are called to holiness, to have the attitude of Christ, and to be like Him.

"We must remove arrogance and pride so we can submit and surrender. Stop trying on your own and completely surrender. Let us humble ourselves as Christians that we may win souls to Christ."
~David Distan

Christ being our Lord, Savior, Brother, and King, still remained humble. He never gave in to the enemy's temptation to gain the world. So, we also must be lowly in heart. Humility transforms and draws us closer to Christ.

THE POWER OF PRAYER

And he said unto me, my grace is sufficient for thee: for my strength is made perfect in weakness. Most gladly therefore will I rather glory in my infirmities, that the power of Christ may rest upon me.
2 Corinthians 12:9

What a privilege we have to commune with our Savior. But how many of us lose out on this precious gift? Christ longs so much to be the first one you run to, to hear your voice, to forgive your repented sins, and to be a part of your family.

When trials and temptations try to destroy you, that's when you use the power of prayer. Every sincere prayer is heard in heaven. The Savior is waiting to make concessions on your behalf to your heavenly Father. Begin depending on the Holy Spirit and the strength of your guardian angel for defense. The Spirit gives you power to overcome. Christ, likewise, eagerly supports us when we depend on Him as our closest Brother.

The enemy is always trying to deceive the mind. Don't let him in. How do we prevent this? With constant prayer! If you do not know how to pray, read a Psalm or repeat the Lord's Prayer in Matthew 6. Try reflecting upon Christ's prayer for you in the Garden of Gethsemane in John 17. The power of prayer is there to empower you and those on whose behalf you intercede. Stay in tune and connected to your Savior. **Surrender your will for His will.** Christ gives peace that the world cannot give.

* **NOTE:** One of the things I enjoy doing is naming my guardian angel. It gives me a more personal connection and a sense of reassurance and comfort.

OUR COMFORTER

Christ, as your Comforter, has molded you and named you. You are His sweet and precious child. Your losses are His losses, your pain, His pain. He knows your deepest desires and your despairs.

It is so sweet that our only hope is in Christ Jesus. Let us not imagine life without Him. How desolate this world would be and even more unbearable our grief. Let us praise our dear Savior for the compassionate and tender love He bestows upon us daily.

For I know that all things work together for good to them that love God, to them who are called according to His purpose. Remember to hold on to the blessed hope He grants us, which brings us peace as we cling closer to our Savior.

POWER OF PRAYER

_____
_____
_____
_____, AMEN!

JOURNAL THOUGHTS

REVENGEFUL

It is no longer I that live, but Christ liveth in me.
Galatians 2:20 (ASV)

SYMPTOMS:

*pride,
rage,
disgruntled,
hateful,
demanding,
self-centered,
selfish,
untrusting,
unloving,
unforgiving*

YOUR CHECK-UP:

HOW ARE YOU FEELING TODAY?

☐ Happy   ☐ Sad   ☐ Anxious
☐ Frustrated   ☐ Stressed   ☐ Angry
☐ Numb   ☐ Overwhelmed

WHY?: _____
_____
_____

WHO IS YOUR GOD?

The story of **Haman** reminds us that through pride, self can become our god that drives us to the point of killing.

In Esther 3:5–9, Mordecai, Esther's uncle, refused to bow down to Haman. So Haman deceived the king and created a law that would not only destroy the one person that offended him (Mordecai), but would destroy his enemy's entire nation. **Would you consider this the ultimate plan of revenge?** Can you relate to Haman?

How many of us have plotted and planned to take revenge on someone that has wronged us? This is the power of letting the enemy feed us negative thoughts. Remember revenge doesn't always come in the form of violence; it can show up as silent treatment, lashing out, or gossip.

REVENGEFUL

VIOLATION OF THE SIXTH COMMANDMENT:

Thou shalt not kill.

Did you know the Bible tells us hate is like murder?

1 John 3:5
Whosoever hateth his brother is a murderer: and ye know that no murderer hath eternal life abiding in him.

Will you allow hate and vengeance to separate you from the love of your heavenly Father?

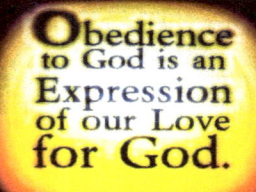

Obedience to God is an Expression of our Love for God.

GOD'S PLAN

What is holding you back from having your peace, your joy? Beware of negative thinking. It can overtake your life and cripple your spiritual growth. When we hold on to anger, hurt, trauma, and unforgiveness, we are tormenting ourselves, and missing out on the blessings God has for us. Many times bitterness festers into physical illness, mental warfare, spiritual battles, and even death. *Do you desire to please your heavenly Father?*

Overcoming is for you, not for others. You are robbing yourself each and every day you do not overcome. This can make it unbearable for others to be around you, as you also miss the special blessings of fellowship.

To enter into God's righteousness and heavenly Home, you must give up all spirits of darkness. Surrender, pray, confess your sins, and repent. The Holy Spirit will give you self-control to change your behavior to reflect Christ's character and become an overcomer.

WHO'S YOUR DICTATOR?

Anger uncontrolled can lead to resentment, bitterness, hate, and finally revenge. What you don't realize is, you are being controlled by the enemy. In your mind you feel as if you are making the decision to pay back those who have hurt, embarrassed, or taken advantage of you. But this is a delusion; you are giving into the flesh, to the offences. Sin begins in the mind (heart). God knows the true intentions and motives of your heart. "…Man looketh on the outward appearance, but the Lord looketh on the heart," (1 Samuel 16:7).

Put your foot down. Don't allow those negative emotions and a spirit of the enemy to continue to dictate your life. You don't have to take matters into your own hand, God repays those who take advantage of His children, and He doesn't give you more than you can handle.

SELF-CONTROL

GIVE IN TO THE POWER OF THE HOLY SPIRIT AND OF SELF-CONTROL.

WE WILL REACH OUR HIGHEST POTENTIAL WHEN WE RELEASE THE DICTATES OF THE FLESH.

WHOM TO FORGIVE?

_____
_____
_____
_____
_____
_____
_____
_____

WARNING: Narcissist Detected!

So how about in the case of a person dictating to you?

You have been created to naturally desire intimacy with your Creator. But instead, you search for it in others, longing for love and a fulfilling connection outside of the Savior. This is impossible! Many times you may end up in the wrong relationship with a person that sees your vulnerabilities and takes disadvantage of you, all while making you feel loved, wanted, and appreciated. Yet, it's done through the deceptions of manipulation, lies, and pain, whether in a friendship or a romantic relationship. This is considered a narcissist. A narcissist doesn't break your heart. They break your spirit.

That is why it takes so long to heal. But lacking a true intimacy with your Savior is the **missing link!**

If you want to understand Narcissistic Personality, let's take a look at the beginning in **Genesis 3:**

- ✓ Satan was calculating
- ✓ Very charming
- ✓ Deceitful of who he really was
- ✓ Offered something that wasn't what he said it was
- ✓ Flattered Eve
- ✓ Had an ulterior motive behind something he portrayed as good
- ✓ Isolated Eve from her husband

SELF-CONTROL

But ye are a chosen generation, a royal priesthood, an holy nation, a peculiar people; that ye should shew forth the praises of Him who hath called you out of darkness into His marvelous light.

1 Peter 2:9

Negative Thoughts
_____
_____
_____
_____
_____
_____

What Satan did was gaslight Eve, to make her second-guess herself, and doubt her perceptions. This is psychological abuse; all he gave her was a painful and traumatic ending. She already knew what good was. But she thought she had found something better outside of God. Then, Satan allowed her to take the fall alone! This is why your relationship with Christ is so vital, allowing you not to be deceived. You must fully place yourself under His protection. Trusting and surrendering daily! If you cannot, you will remain unfulfilled until you choose to submit to your Savior. **Give God Full Control!**

SURRENDER EVERYTHING ...

As a man thinks in his heart, so is he. I have surely been guilty of wanting revenge. I remember a time in my youth when my anger grew and grew because I kept in my emotions for far too long. It festered into an ugly monster that was inside. Because of this, I blamed the person that was the target of my anger instead of taking responsibility.

I did not speak up earlier to resolve the irritation. Instead, I allowed it to brew and brew. I exploded and created an embarrassing situation. Thoughts of revenge, shame, and rage developed, so someone had to pay!

When you believe in God, you accept His words as truth, so stay humble and surrender all your will to Him. When you misrepresent your Savior's character to others, you are held accountable for being that person's stumbling block. But remember, angels of God are waiting to show you the correct path of life. You can surrender to God's control or choose to do it on your own.

SELF-CONTROL

AFTER TIME WITH CHRIST:

HOW DO YOU FEEL?

☐ Happy ☐ Sad ☐ Anxious
☐ Frustrated ☐ Stressed ☐ Angry
☐ Numb ☐ Content ☐ Peaceful

COMMENT: _____
_____
_____

Christ, Our Example …

Our greatest obstacle is lack of self-control, which Christ overcame in the wilderness (see Matt. 4:4). Still, you must decide if you'll choose the path of righteousness or of self. Do you expect to live a sinful life on Earth and then be allowed to enter into a **sinless heaven?** As the apostle Paul states: "**God forbid!**" (Rom. 6:15).

However, Psalm 34:16 reminds us that the Lord is against anyone that does evil. We must overcome as He did before we can enter into His kingdom. As Christians, we will be tested if we are truly walking with Christ. But, there is a beautiful reward in heaven. Imagine when you are forever with Him. There is victory over your life. I encourage you to stay steadfast and faithful. **It's worth the wait!**

FROM GOD:
PEACE I GIVE TO YOU, NOT AS THE WORLD GIVES YOU!

Your Prayer

_____
_____
_____
_____, AMEN!

PERFECTED CHARACTER

GALATIANS 6:8 *"For he that soweth to his flesh shall of the flesh reap corruption; but he that soweth to the Spirit shall of the Spirit reap life everlasting."*

PERFECTED CHARACTER

Does this seem impossible?
Are you ready to perfect your character? Character development is a lifelong work. *Philippians 1:11* teaches us about the fruits of righteousness, which is *love* authored by Christ. There are only two fruits we can bear: *love* or *selfishness*. A perfect character should display the fruits of the spirit: unity, sympathy, mercy, and forgiveness. A reflection of **Christ!**

THE ADVERSARY

The closer we draw to Christ, the closer we draw to God and the closer we come to each other. This is how we attain love, not trying to get closer to others, but to Christ.

Always remember, the enemy does not want you to win nor to experience peace. Behold Him who is love, and you will be transformed.
"Love seeks not her own way" (see 1 Cor. 13:5).

OVERCOMING

The reason you struggle to forgive others and even yourself is because the offense takes residence in your mind. You continue to replay this hurt over and over, which keeps it alive.

Surrender the negative thoughts of what others have done to you, so that unforgiveness and anger can pass away. 1 Peter 4:8 (NLT) tells, *"Love covers a multitude of sins."* Keep the good of others continually before you. Let your light so shine for Christ, as you surrender to achieve His perfection. *"Love worketh no ill to his neighbor: therefore love is the fulfilling of the law"* (Rom. 13:10).

OBEDIENCE

Obedience is an expression of love by willfully following the laws of God. Hebrews 1:9 tells us when we love righteousness, we will hate iniquity (which is sin or wrong-doing).

We are all guilty of not following the laws accordingly. This is not due to not having enough strength to resist sin, but not enough love for the Savior. Let us keep the laws out of love, not obligation or fear. We will then experience a true freedom. Memorize for moments of weakness, (Psalm 119:11), *"Thy word have I hid in my heart that I might not sin against Thee."*

SURRENDER RECIPE

1. Contemplate daily who God is!
2. Spend a thoughtful hour each morning with Christ.
3. Only when you receive Christ, the author of love, can you fulfill your greatest need for love.
4. Merge yourself into Christ. Submit your heart to Him, and love will spring forth constantly.
5. **PRAYER:** Father, help us to develop this love in our homes, so we can bring it to our church and take it to the world.

OUR PRAYER

Father, we are lacking in love because we do not look to Christ. We are no longer contemplating His marvelous sacrifice nor seeing the price sin has cost Him. I am pleading, dear Father, that you kindly help us. Place us in circumstances where this love can develop. Help us to hold fast while our characters are being molded.

Please remove pride and show us how to be meek and lowly in heart as Christ. Thank You for Your willingness Father, to give us this **Love**.

JOURNAL THOUGHTS

PRAYERLIST

Day 1:_____
Day 2:_____
Day 3:_____
Day 4:_____
Day 5:_____
Day 6:_____
Day 7:_____
Day 8:_____
Day 9:_____
Day 10:_____
Day 11:_____
Day 12:_____
Day 13:_____
Day 14:_____
Day 15:_____
Day 16:_____
Day 17:_____
Day 18:_____
Day 19:_____
Day 20:_____
Day 21:_____
Day 22:_____
Day 23:_____
Day 24:_____
Day 25:_____
Day 26:_____
Day 27:_____
Day 28:_____
Day 29:_____
Day 30:_____

ANSWERED PRAYERS

#1:_____ #12:_____

#2:_____ #13:_____

#3:_____ #14:_____

#4:_____ #15:_____

#5:_____ #16:_____

#6:_____ #17:_____

#7:_____ #18:_____

#8:_____ #19:_____

#9:_____ #20:_____

#10:_____ #21:_____

#11:_____ #22:_____

REFLECTIVE THOUGHTS

You have been SAVED to SAVE!

I pray your journey has been a blessing, and your **love for Christ** has grown deeper during these daily devotions. Christ is waiting and wanting to be your best supporter, your greatest ally, and your closest friend.

Christ submitted His will to His Father in the Garden of Gethsemane. Let us follow in His footsteps of willful obedience, without compromise.

Trust Christ to help you through this journey. Remember, character development is a lifelong work. Hold on tightly to Him as He does a refining work in and through you.

THE FRUIT OF SALVATION!

When we experience spiritual death (numbness), this is evidence of cherished spiritual pride, which leads us to a stunted Christian walk. This may seem like a small sin, but oftentimes, Satan uses this to fulfill his mission. Sin is so sweet when we are on the enemy's side that it seems he no longer troubles us since we are now working in partnership with him. The fruit of the Spirit is evidence of salvation. So are you living for the reason you were made? **It is to know God and glorify Him!**

"It is imperative that we employ the fruit of the Spirit in our daily Christian walk. The Holy Spirit has given us nine perfect nutrients (love, joy, peace, patience, kindness, goodness, faith, humility, self-control) within the fruit to give us hope against the enemy's attacks. In this constant battle of being led by our flesh or by the Spirit, we must give our lives to God so that the Spirit's fruit can flourish and ripen inside of us. Only then can God begin to work in and through us to make us more like Jesus." ~Kari Hart

You have been **SAVED** to bring others who are hurting to God! Rely on Him earnestly, so you can begin our mission for Christ.

ECCLESIASTES 12:13–14
Fear God, and keep His commandments: for this is the whole duty of man, for God shall bring every work into judgment.

GRATITUDE

NOTES

EARNEST SCRIPTURE & SONG

HEBREWS 4:12

¹² For the word of God is quick, and powerful, and sharper than any twoedged sword, piercing even to the dividing asunder of soul and spirit, and of the joints and marrow, and is a discerner of the thoughts and intents of the heart.

¹² For the word of God is quick, and powerful, and sharper than any twoedged sword, piercing even to the dividing asunder of soul and spirit, and of the joints and marrow, and is a discerner of the thoughts and intents of the heart.

The word God is powerful.

~ Hebrews 4:12
https://www.youtube.com/watch?v=0wv790_fXFM

SOLEMN SCRIPTURE & SONG

ISAIAH 4:16, 19-20

[16] Bind up the testimony, seal the law among my disciples. (2x)

[20] To the law and to the testimony: if they speak not according to this word, it is because there is no light in them. (2x)

[19] And when they shall say unto you, Seek unto them that have familiar spirits, and unto wizards that peep, and that mutter: should not a people seek unto their God? for the living to the dead?

[0] To the law and to the testimony: if they speak not according to this word, it is because there is no light in them.

[0] To the law and to the testimony: if they speak not according to this word, it is because there is no light in them.

[20] To the law and to the testimony: if they speak not according to this word, it is because there is no light in them. (repeat)

~ Isaiah 4:16, 19-20
https://www.youtube.com/watch?v=N01PA0Yk8e8

HEARTFELT SCRIPTURE & SONG

REVELATION 21: 4-7

⁴ And God shall wipe away all tears from their eyes; and there shall be no more death, neither sorrow, nor crying, neither shall there be any more pain: for the former things are passed away.

⁶ And he said unto me, It is done. I am Alpha and Omega, the beginning and the end. I will give unto him that is athirst of the fountain of the water of life freely.

⁵ And he that sat upon the throne said, Behold, I make all things new. And he said unto me, Write: for these words are true and faithful.

⁶ And he said unto me, It is done. I am Alpha and Omega, the beginning and the end. I will give unto him that is athirst of the fountain of the water of life freely.

⁷ He that overcometh shall inherit all things; and I will be his God, and he shall be my son.

⁶ And he said unto me, It is done. I am Alpha and Omega, the beginning and the end. I will give unto him that is athirst of the fountain of the water of life freely.

~ Revelation 21:4–7
https://www.youtube.com/watch?v=hdvQVtITYYo

REFLECTIVE SCRIPTURE & SONG

THE BLESSED HOPE

[13] But I would not have you to be ignorant, brethren, concerning them which are asleep, that ye sorrow not, even as others which have no hope.

[14] For if we believe that Jesus died and rose again, even so them also which sleep in Jesus will God bring with him, will God bring with him.

[15] For this we say unto you by the word of the Lord, that we which are alive and remain unto the coming of the Lord shall not prevent them which are asleep.

[16] For the Lord himself shall descend from heaven with a shout, with the voice of the archangel, and with the trump of God, trump of God: and the dead in Christ shall rise first:

[17] Then we which are alive and remain shall be caught up together with them in the clouds, to meet the Lord in the air: and so shall we ever be with the Lord, so shall we ever be with the Lord.

FOREVER, BE WITH THE LORD!

~ 1 Thessalonians 4:13–17
https://www.youtube.com/watch?v=bP2yILnm4SQ

ADDITIONAL RESOURCES

CRYING FOR HELP!

In your moments of darkness,
I plead for you to hold on just a little longer.
Don't Give Up & Don't Give In!

I recall walking on top of a bridge after listening to the enemy, tears running down my face uncontrollably. Feeling numb and done with life, I stood there contemplating. A few minutes later, a truck driver honked his horn at me and waved. I broke down even more in tears because I knew God had sent an angel that day to save me. He wanted me to know that He loved me and cared.

Daily the enemy tells us so many lies, ones that seem truthful at times. His mission is to have us deceived and lost, so we may perish alongside him on the **Day of Judgment.**

****

God's love for you is so profoundly grand. His purpose for you is unfathomable; you simply have not heard Him calling for you.
Your heavenly Father longs for you to hear His voice. To know His marvelous will for your life. Remove the distractions of the world, unfulfilled relationships, negative friends, your destructive thoughts, and listen more carefully. When you hear God's voice, it erases the lies the enemy whispers about you.

IF YOU ARE IN NEED OF SUPPORT…

1. Please call the Suicide Hotline at 800.273.8255. Anytime! To speak with an advisor.

2. If you are in need of a support group or more. Visit afsp.org for immediate HELP!

GOD DOES NOT DESIRE YOU TO SUFFER ALONE.
WE ARE HERE TO HELP EACH OTHER AND TO DISCOVER
THE HOPE OF HIS SOON
RETURN & HEAVENLY KINGDOM!

NOTES

JOIN THE JOURNEY: inspiretolivenow.com

NOTES

TEACH Services, Inc.
PUBLISHING

We invite you to view the complete
selection of titles we publish at:
www.TEACHServices.com

We encourage you to write us
with your thoughts about this,
or any other book we publish at:
info@TEACHServices.com

TEACH Services' titles may be purchased in
bulk quantities for educational, fund-raising,
business, or promotional use.
bulksales@TEACHServices.com

Finally, if you are interested in seeing
your own book in print, please contact us at:
publishing@TEACHServices.com

We are happy to review your manuscript at no charge.

www.ingramcontent.com/pod-product-compliance
Lightning Source LLC
Chambersburg PA
CBHW060925170426

43192CB00024B/2899